ULTRA
HUSH-HUSH

ESPIONAGE AND
SPECIAL MISSIONS

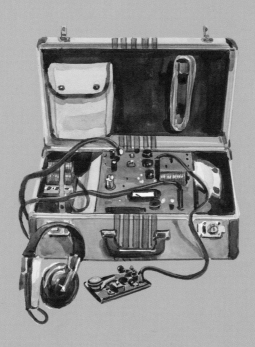

BY STEPHEN SHAPIRO AND TINA FORRESTER

ART BY DAVID CRAIG

ANNICK PRESS

TORONTO • NEW YORK • VANCOUVER

Book and cover design: Sheryl Shapiro
Image research: Sandra Booth
Photograph credits appear at the back of the book.

We acknowledge the support of the Canada Council for the Arts, the Ontario Arts Council, and the Government of Canada through the Book Publishing Industry Development Program (BPIDP) for our publishing activities.

Cataloging in Publication Data

Shapiro, Stephen, date-
    Ultra hush-hush : espionage and special missions / by Stephen Shapiro and Tina Forrester ; illustrated by David Craig.

(Outwitting the enemy : stories from the second World War)
Includes index.
ISBN 1-55037-779-5 (bound).—ISBN 1-55037-778-7 (pbk.)

1. World War, 1939-1945—Secret service—Juvenile literature. 2. World War, 1939-1945—Deception—Juvenile literature. 3. World War, 1939-1945—Cryptography—Juvenile literature. I. Forrester, Tina II. Craig, David III. Title. IV. Series.

D810.S7S48 2003   j940.54'85   C2002-904998-9

The art in this book was rendered in oils.
The text was typeset in New Baskerville, Serpentine, and Myriad.

Distributed in Canada by:
Firefly Books Ltd.
3680 Victoria Park Avenue
Willowdale, ON
M2H 3K1

Published in the U.S.A. by Annick Press (U.S.) Ltd.
Distributed in the U.S.A. by:
Firefly Books (U.S.) Inc.
P.O. Box 1338
Ellicott Station
Buffalo, NY 14205

Printed and bound in Canada by Friesens, Altona, Manitoba.

Visit us at: www.annickpress.com

Those who forget history are
doomed to repeat it.
—George Santayana

The world of spies is the world of secrets. Sometimes it is hard
to know the difference between true stories and false. Novels
and movies about spies, full of action and adventure, are mostly
how we understand this mysterious world of espionage. But
historians like to say that truth can be stranger than fiction.
Truth can also be just as exciting. The stories contained in *Ultra
Hush-hush* take us back to World War II, one of the most
important wars in history. These stories are about spies and
saboteurs and about the impact their lives had on the outcome
of the war. They are exciting stories, but true, and they tell us
something we need to know. Spies are not just James Bond
figures, but real people who risk their lives to protect what they
believe in. We now live in a world in which we hear about
terrorists and spies and the role of espionage on almost a daily
basis. To help us understand the secrets of today, we can look
back on the secrets of a war in which espionage did so
much to achieve victory.

Professor Wesley K. Wark,
Department of History, University of Toronto
Intelligence and National Security, co-editor
The Oxford Companion to Modern Espionage, editor-in-chief

TIMELINE

1939 Germany invades Poland (September 1)

Britain and France declare war on Germany (September 3)

1940 Germany invades Norway (April 9)

Germany invades France, Belgium, Holland (May 10)

Italy declares war on Allies (June 10)

1941 Germany invades USSR (June 22)

Japan attacks Pearl Harbor (December 7)

Japan invades the Philippines (December 10)

1942 Battle of Coral Sea (May 7–8)

Battle of Midway (June 3–6)

Battle of El Alamein, Egypt, begins (October 23)

1943 Italy surrenders (September 3)

Germans capture Rome (September 10)

1944 Allies capture Rome (June 4)

D-Day (June 6)

1945 President Roosevelt dies (April 12)

Germany surrenders (May 7)

Bombing of Hiroshima (August 6)

Bombing of Nagasaki (August 9)

Japan officially surrenders (September 2)

D-DAY: the Allied invasion of Normandy, France, on June 6, 1944, that led to the liberation of France and the invasion of Germany

On D-Day, American troops storm ashore on the coast of France.

CONTENTS

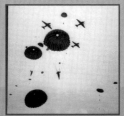

WWII parachutists

British tank, Eighth Army, Libya

Bicycles were confiscated in Rembrandt Square, Amsterdam, in front of German headquarters. The Dutch were then handed receipts saying "Payable after German Victory Day."

A WORLD AT WAR

ALLIES:
the alliance during the Second World War that included Great Britain, the United States, Canada, Australia, India, New Zealand, South Africa, the U.S.S.R., China, and many other countries.

AXIS:
the alliance during the Second World War made up of Germany, Italy, Japan, Hungary, Bulgaria, Romania, and Finland.

AXIS OCCUPIED:
Countries occupied by the Axis during the Second World War included France, Belgium, the Netherlands, Denmark, Norway, Poland, Greece, Yugoslavia, the Philippines, and many others.

NEUTRAL:
Countries that remained neutral during the Second World War included Sweden, Switzerland, Portugal, Ireland, Spain, and Turkey.

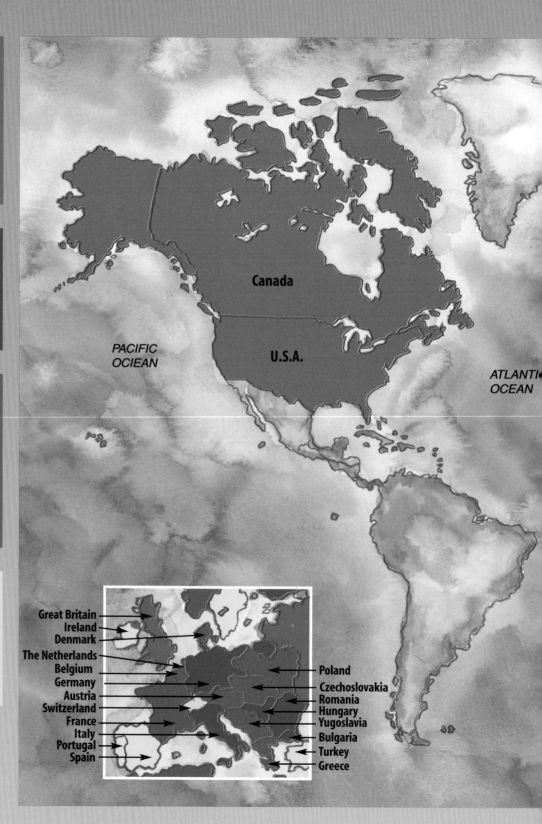

Canada

PACIFIC OCIEAN

U.S.A.

ATLANTIC OCEAN

Great Britain
Ireland
Denmark
The Netherlands
Belgium
Germany
Austria
Switzerland
France
Italy
Portugal
Spain

Poland
Czechoslovakia
Romania
Hungary
Yugoslavia
Bulgaria
Turkey
Greece

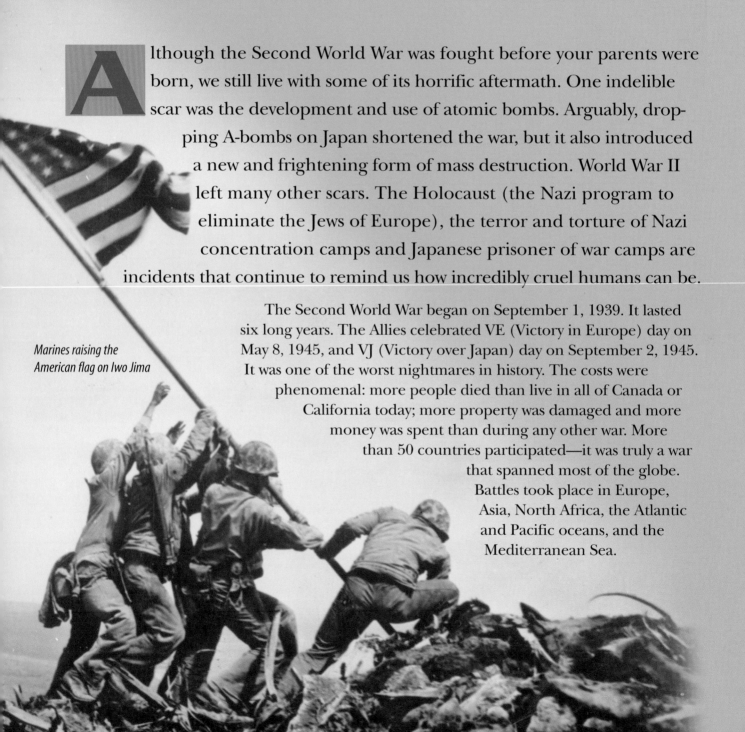

INTRODUCTION

Although the Second World War was fought before your parents were born, we still live with some of its horrific aftermath. One indelible scar was the development and use of atomic bombs. Arguably, dropping A-bombs on Japan shortened the war, but it also introduced a new and frightening form of mass destruction. World War II left many other scars. The Holocaust (the Nazi program to eliminate the Jews of Europe), the terror and torture of Nazi concentration camps and Japanese prisoner of war camps are incidents that continue to remind us how incredibly cruel humans can be.

Marines raising the American flag on Iwo Jima

The Second World War began on September 1, 1939. It lasted six long years. The Allies celebrated VE (Victory in Europe) day on May 8, 1945, and VJ (Victory over Japan) day on September 2, 1945. It was one of the worst nightmares in history. The costs were phenomenal: more people died than live in all of Canada or California today; more property was damaged and more money was spent than during any other war. More than 50 countries participated—it was truly a war that spanned most of the globe. Battles took place in Europe, Asia, North Africa, the Atlantic and Pacific oceans, and the Mediterranean Sea.

Children sitting outside their bombed-out home in London

Probably the world should have seen war coming. There were warnings. Throughout the 1930s—the decade that led to the Second World War—power-hungry nations such as Japan, Italy, and Germany began to rearm and expand their borders. Other nations stood by, seemingly helpless to act. It was the time of the Great Depression, when many governments were preoccupied with high unemployment, the jobless, and hungry citizens within their own borders. The Western democracies, above all, did not want a repeat of the bloodletting of the First World War.

Then a jolt came on September 1, 1939: German forces invaded Poland and destroyed its armed forces in a matter of weeks. Now it was clear that the German leader, Adolf Hitler, a ruthless and dangerous man, wanted most of Europe. Countries other than those being invaded began taking sides. Two days after the lightning-fast invasion of Poland, the Allies (Great Britain, France, Australia, India, and New Zealand) declared war on Germany. Within the next week, South Africa and Canada joined the Allies.

Germany had been preparing for war. Its armies were trained and German factories were equipped to make war materials. The

German troops march through Warsaw, Poland, 1939

Allies, on the other hand, were unprepared. During 1940 and 1941, German armies conquered countries to its north, south, east, and west: Denmark, Norway, Belgium, the Netherlands, Luxembourg, France, Greece, and Yugoslavia. The Germans bombed Great Britain and tried to cut off British supplies arriving by ship. But the British fought back with all their resources. When Germany invaded the Union of Soviet Socialist Republics (U.S.S.R., also called Russia) on June 22, 1941, the Russians joined the war against Hitler. Meanwhile, Italy, Bulgaria, Hungary, Romania, and Finland sided with Germany. This group formed the Axis, an alliance that seemed almost impossible to defeat.

By the end of 1941, only two major world powers were not at war: Japan and the United States. That changed when Japan— which had signed a military alliance with Germany and Italy in 1940—attacked the

U.S. naval base at Pearl Harbor, Hawaii. The U.S. immediately declared war on Japan. Germany declared war on the U.S. three days later. All the world's powerful nations were now at war.

The war brought six years of terror, hatred, and cruelty. But difficult circumstances can inspire innovation and creativity. The accounts in this book demonstrate that some people show great resourcefulness under pressure. The stickier the problem, the more creative they become. For instance, when the Japanese planned to knock the Americans out of the war, a code breaker at Pearl Harbor tricked the Japanese into confirming that Midway was their next secret target. And when "Black Devil" Tom Prince's telephone wires were severed, he performed a clever ruse to get his message through—even though the Germans were watching every move he made. You want these people on your side during a war!

ESPIONAGE

Tales about the fictional character James Bond, agent 007, contain at least three truths: nations do spy on one another; espionage is dangerous; and spy stories can be riveting.

Governments hire spies for many reasons. Often they want to collect military, industrial, or political information to help protect their citizens. For example, if a country were suddenly to amass a huge army, its neighbors would want to learn about it as soon as possible in order to defend themselves.

Sometimes spies look for intelligence that could give their country an advantage over other nations. When the Americans began the Manhattan Project to develop the atomic bomb, they took extraordinary precautions to keep their secrets out of the hands of Nazi spies. If they had failed, the world would be very different now.

Most of the information that spies provided was in the form of copies of secret documents, either papers they came across as part of their job or documents they stole. Some spies traveled, reporting on which ships were in port or what military units were on the move. They sent this information home by letter or secret radio.

People become spies with all kinds of motives. Juan Pujol Garcia became an agent because he wanted to change the political situation in his country, Spain. Eddie Chapman saw an opportunity to get out of prison, and he couldn't resist a good adventure. Elyesa Bazna did it for greed. All three spies lived intriguing lives that took fascinating twists and turns.

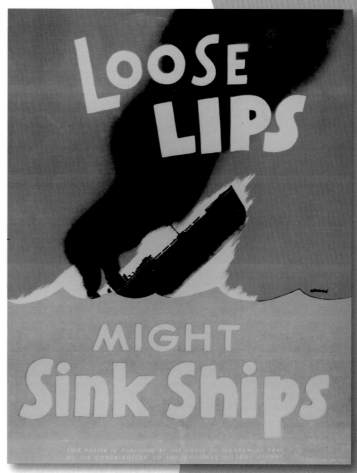

LOOSE LIPS MIGHT Sink Ships

TOP SECRET

THE DOUBLE CROSS SYSTEM

"In wartime, truth is so precious that she should always be attended by a bodyguard of lies."
— **Sir Winston Churchill,**
British prime minister during most of the Second World War

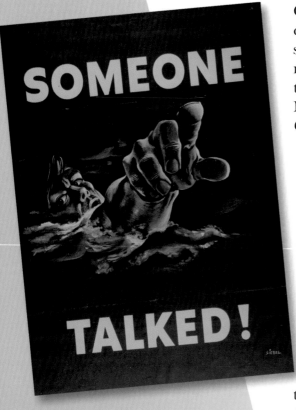

Many battles are won with brute force, but sometimes a weaker foe can gain the edge by discovering beforehand what its opponent is planning. It's common practice for countries to use secret agents in order to keep tabs on what's happening inside and outside their borders. One of the most effective spy operations of all time occurred during the Second World War.

The British Double Cross system was amazingly effective against the Nazis. Although there were more than a hundred German secret agents stationed in Great Britain over the course of the war, the British identified every one. Brilliant sleuthing! But the real coup was that Double Cross turned many of the spies into double agents—spies who pretended to work for the Nazis while actually working for the British. Most of the news the Germans received from their spies in Great Britain was what the British wanted them to hear.

Although it didn't seem a momentous event at the time, the British got their first break early in the war when they arrested Arthur Owens, known to be in contact by mail with the Germans. When Owens—later code-named Snow—volunteered the information that the Nazis had given him a two-way radio, British agents allowed him to maintain contact with the Abwehr ... but under their control. Soon the British discovered through encrypted messages that other Nazi spies were being sent to Great Britain. One by one, the British picked them off. They imprisoned most, executed 13, and turned more than 40 into double agents.

The group responsible for watching over the double agents was the Double Cross Committee, also known as the Twenty Committee because the Roman numerals for 20 (XX) form a double cross. Each double agent was assigned a case officer, allowing the British to figure out what the Germans were planning from the questions Nazi controllers were asking. It also helped them supply the Nazis with false information, along with just enough truth to make the answers seem believable.

Misinformation can really confuse an enemy!

In 1944, three of Double Cross's double agents (their code names: Garbo, Brutus, and Bronx) carried out a masterful deception that allowed the Allies to successfully invade Normandy—the invasion that eventually drove the Nazis out of France. (See Garbo's story, Award Performance, page 13.)

ABWEHR: the German Military Intelligence Service and espionage organization

AWARD PERFORMANCE

GREAT BRITAIN

PAS DE CALAIS

NORMANDY

FRANCE

PORTUGAL

SPAIN

Lisbon

Some liars get away with telling falsehoods, and a few even earn awards for it. During the Second World War, both the Allies and the Axis rewarded successful liars who helped them win battles. And one especially gifted storyteller—Juan Pujol Garcia—was rewarded by both sides!

Garcia loved his home country, Spain, but he hated Francisco Franco, his country's dictator. The Nazis had helped Franco take over Spain in the mid-1930s. Garcia reasoned that if the Allies could topple the Nazis, the Franco government might collapse too. To help make this happen, he decided to spy for Great Britain.

Right off the bat, Garcia's plan hit a snag—the British rejected his offer to work for them. However, Garcia was still determined to help the Allies. In a sly move, he approached the Nazis, and the Germans accepted! They trained him, provided him with money and secret inks, and gave him addresses of contacts and safe lodging in England.

On the way to his assignment, Garcia decided, without permission, to stay in Portugal. (See Den of Spies, this page.) However, he pretended to be in England, writing phony intelligence reports, masterpieces of invention that he created in his head. He did this even though he knew very little about England, concocting his stories from bits of information he gleaned from a map of Great Britain, an old tour guide, newsreels, and even an out-of-date railway timetable. His stories were very believable, and although his reports bore Portuguese postmarks, he made up a story for that too. He claimed that his messages were sent to Portugal by courier, then posted. The Nazis never suspected the truth.

Garcia's act was so convincing, in fact, that the British, who were secretly reading much of the Abwehr's (German intelligence) communications, were also impressed with his "espionage." Of course, they knew he was lying. They asked the Spaniard to work for Double Cross so he wouldn't tell the truth by mistake. (See The Double Cross System, page 12.) Joining Double Cross was what Garcia had wanted in the first place! In April 1942, British intelligence smuggled him into England and eventually gave him the code name Garbo, after

DEN OF SPIES

Portugal was a neutral nation during the Second World War, so Allied, Axis, and neutral countries established intelligence agencies in Lisbon, Portugal's capital. The city's location was perfect. From Lisbon, agents could sail to any seaport. They could also fly to any major city. Or they could sneak across the mountains between Portugal and Spain and then into Nazi-occupied France.

MI5

MI5 (also known as the Security Service) stands for Military Intelligence, section 5. It's a government organization responsible for British national security and counter-espionage. The Double Cross Committee grew out of MI5.

MI6

MI6 (also known as the Secret Intelligence Service, or SIS) stands for Military Intelligence, section 6. It's a government organization responsible for gathering, outside of Great Britain, any intelligence that concerns British vital interests.

Hollywood's famous Greta Garbo, another convincing actor, who had portrayed a famous World War I secret agent onscreen.

By war's end, Garcia's vivid imagination, aided by British intelligence, had invented a network of more than 20 informants who supposedly gave him a constant stream of information about British war preparations. He sent this information by British-controlled radio to the 90—mostly misinformation, of course, sprinkled with a few truths to make his messages sound plausible.

Garcia's most significant ruse occurred on June 6, 1944. The Germans already suspected that the Allies were about to invade Nazi-occupied France, probably crossing the English Channel to invade Pas de Calais or the beaches on the Normandy peninsula. But they didn't know when or exactly where.

Aware that Garcia was trusted by high-ranking Nazis, including Hitler, the Double Cross Committee (see The Double Cross System, page 12) had him send accurate information to the 90, warning German intelligence that Allied soldiers were about to invade Normandy. The trick was to make sure that the message was delayed, arriving in German hands only after the invasion forces had landed. A later transmission suggested that the Normandy invasion was merely a decoy operation and that the real invasion was yet to come. This caused the Germans to stop important reinforcements from going to Normandy in anticipation of a much larger invasion at Pas de Calais by a totally fictional army assembled in southeast England.

For his contribution to the war, the British government made Garcia a Member of the Order of the British Empire (MBE). And for his services to Hitler, the Germans awarded him the Iron Cross (see page 16) … because, even at the end of the war, the Germans still believed that Garcia was working for them. Now that's fine acting!

IMAGINARY SPIES IN CANADA

If an agent didn't pass on information he should have been able to obtain, the Germans suspected he was really a double agent working for the British. Garbo wanted to stay on good terms with the Nazis, so some of his imaginary sub-agents were "sent" to Canada so they would be unable to see things Double Cross didn't want reported. Usually, the reason given was that the agent was fleeing the police.

GARBO'S NETWORK

Garbo invented four sub-agents while he was working in Portugal:

Agent One – a Portuguese traveler
Agent Two – a German-Swiss businessman, who Garbo claimed died of cancer before he could observe convoys he should have been able to see out his window
Agent Three – a rich South American who supposedly had three sources of his own in Scotland
J-1 – the courier who took Garbo's reports to Lisbon

By February 1944, Garbo had 24 imaginary sources. When Garbo's network's radio traffic grew too heavy for him to encipher, he hired Agent Two's widow. (Of course, in reality, MI5 helped him.) Here are a few more of the agents he made up:

Agent Four – a waiter from Gibraltar who worked in a military club and had three sub-agents of his own, one of whom worked Garbo's radio transmitter
Agent Five – an informer who moved to Canada, which turned out to be a convenient place to send agents on the run
Agent Six – another fictitious agent who died, this one in a plane crash
Agent Seven – an ex-sailor who was a member of the imaginary organization called Brothers of the Aryan World Order

Officer of the Order of the British Empire

THE BLUE DIVISION

Although Spain never officially joined the Second World War, Franco did feel obliged to assist the Nazis in return for German support during the Spanish Civil War, the upheaval that had led to his dictatorship. Franco also wanted to punish the Russians, who had supported his opponents. So, in 1941, he formed the Blue Division—named for the blue uniforms the troops wore when not in German service—and sent them off to the Russian front to help the Nazis. While serving on the Russian front, Spanish soldiers were eligible for German decorations, including the Iron Cross.

Since Garbo was not a soldier, he was enrolled in the Blue Division (although he never actually served in it) in order that he could receive an Iron Cross.

THE IRON CROSS

Rich in tradition, the German Iron Cross dates back to 1813, when the medal was first awarded to courageous Prussians who had fought valiantly against Napoleon's advancing French armies. Its three ranks (2nd Class, 1st Class, and above these the Grand Cross) were also the highest German military decorations awarded during both the Franco-Prussian War and the First World War. During the Second World War, Hitler expanded the number of ranks to eight, inserting five levels of the Knight's Cross between 1st Class and the Grand Cross.

Iron Cross 2nd Class

Hitler had been awarded the Iron Cross 1st Class and 2nd Class during the First World War. He was keenly aware of how the medal bolstered nationalistic feelings among Germans. It was presented for remarkable bravery, exceptional war planning, outstanding leadership, and general merit to military persons and uniformed civilians (such as policemen, firemen, or Hitler Youth).

Traditionally, the Iron Cross 2nd Class was won before the 1st Class (the lower grade before the higher), though occasionally the 1st and 2nd were awarded at the same time. During the Second World War, only one person received the Grand Cross: Hermann Göring (commander-in-chief of the German air force).

THE ORDER OF THE BRITISH EMPIRE

In 1917, King George V created the Order of the British Empire to recognize the contribution to the war effort of servicemen in non-combatant positions. In 1918, the Order was expanded to include civilians.

It was the first British order of chivalry to include women, though only the first two levels actually bestow knighthood: Knight (or Dame) Grand Cross and Knight (or Dame) Commander. The three lower ranks are Commander, Officer, and Member.

The Order at any level was awarded for gallantry (heroic courage) or services to the Empire at home, in India, or in the Dominions and colonies. It is awarded to foreigners as well as British subjects.

CROOK TURNED SPY

Eddie Chapman was a thief, but he was not a traitor … even though he convinced the Nazis that he was. The truth was that Chapman had a scheming mind, and in 1940 he wanted to get out of jail. Telling the Germans he would spy for them gained him his freedom.

Chapman had been a British safecracker. He was so well known when he escaped from a Scottish jail in 1939 that he had to sneak out of Great Britain to avoid being caught again. He and his gang chose to hide on Jersey, one of the Channel Islands—owned by England but located only about 10 miles (16 km) from the French coast. The law might not have discovered their hiding place except one of the gang members made a big mistake: he sent his girlfriend a letter that helped the police track them down.

When the Germans occupied the Channel Islands in 1940, Chapman was in a Jersey jail. He wanted out, so he concocted a story for the Germans and soon discovered that persuading them he was a malcontent was easy. All he had to do was explain that he had a police record and mention he was a deserter from the Coldstream Guards. This was all true. For added punch, he threw in a few lies about how much he hated Great Britain because he had been denied a good education, a plight that forced him into a life of crime. The Germans thought Chapman was interested in revenge and that lining his pockets with money would turn him into just the kind of person they could use.

Astonishingly, the Germans executed Chapman! Well, not really. Actually, they moved him to a prison in occupied France, where he was supposedly shot by a firing squad, a ruse to convince the British that he was now dead. Then he was taken to Germany, where he learned some German and was trained in sabotage and radio techniques.

In December 1942, Fritz—Chapman's German code name—parachuted into England equipped with a radio, a pistol, a cyanide suicide pill (in case he was caught), and £1,000. He landed in a field, walked into town, and turned himself in. MI5 had intercepted secret messages and were waiting for him. They accepted the former

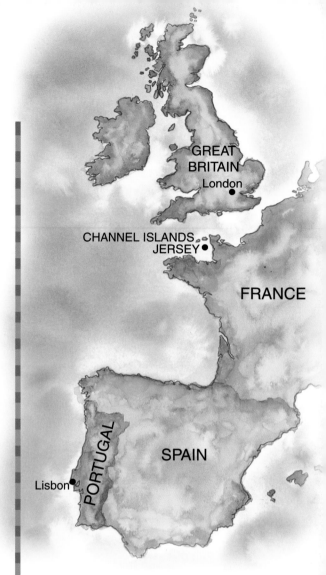

COLDSTREAM GUARDS

Her Majesty's Coldstream Regiment of Foot Guards has distinguished itself in many British battles and is one of the most prestigious infantry regiments in the British army. Some members of the regiment guard London's Buckingham Palace wearing red tunics and tall black bearskin hats.

£: the symbol for the British currency, the pound

DESERTER: someone who leaves the army without permission

MASKELYNE AND HIS "MAGIC GANG"

Major Jasper Maskelyne and his Magic Gang were members of a British army unit that specialized in creating amazing illusions. During the Desert War in Egypt (1941–42), they he... fo... ev... pu... Ge... va... th...

[handwritten note overlays text:] He was a safe breaker + was used to using explosives, so they wanted him to blow up the Mosquito fighter plane factory in Britian. Used canvas on roof, blow up dummies on the ground

Th... of... m... Ma... as... of... na...

being fired at. The pilots dropped their bombs on the phony harbor and flew back to their base.

The Magic Gang also hid the Suez Canal, the man-made waterway in Egypt that connects European and Asian ports. To make the canal vanish, the gang built a series of spinning strobe lights. The pulsing lights disoriented German pilots so they didn't know where to drop their bombs.

Another clever ruse was carried out in the desert south of El Alamein. Maskelyne and his men created a phantom army. They used wood, cardboard, and canvas to make guns, tanks, and other war machinery that tricked Rommel, the German general, into thinking the British Eighth Army was about to attack from the south when they were really coming from the north.

> **BRASS: military slang for high-ranking officers who have brass-colored braid in their caps**

crook's offer to work for Double Cross and rechristened him Zig Zag! (See The Double Cross System, page 12.)

Chapman's mission for the Germans was an almost impossible one: he was supposed to blow up the de Havilland Aircraft Works north of London, where the Mosquito was being built. (See de Havilland, page 20.) Chapman realized he needed to carry out his mission to prove his worth to the Germans—but how could he blow up the factory without affecting aircraft production? Double Cross had a solution. They called in some professionals to create the illusion that the plant had been destroyed with explosives. This was the perfect story since Chapman had often used explosives as a safecracker.

The professionals—Major Jasper Maskelyne and his Magic Gang—painted a gigantic canvas the size of the factory's powerhouse roof to make it look like the roof had gaping holes through which damage could be seen inside the building. About two months after Chapman parachuted into England, Maskelyne and his men scattered papier mâché dummies that looked like blown-up generators along with bricks, blocks, and other debris around the plant. Then Chapman radioed his German contact that he had completed his mission.

A German reconnaissance plane flew over to check his work, and the canvas looked so real that they reported he had indeed blown up the de Havilland factory. Chapman's controller congratulated him. Double Cross was pleased too. They put Chapman on a British ship bound for Portugal so he could make his way back to France for further missions.

A German representative in Lisbon, where the ship docked in Portugal, offered Chapman a large sum of money if he would place a piece of "coal" on the ship he had just arrived on. He accepted the job. The "coal" turned out to be an explosive designed to detonate when it was placed in a fire. But it never caused any damage. Instead of placing

DE HAVILLAND

De Havilland was the aircraft manufacturing company that designed and built the twin-engine Mosquito, a plane that could be used in various roles. When the Mosquito was equipped with guns and bombs, it was used as a fighter-bomber for low-level ground attacks. Outfitted with radar, it was used as a night fighter to hunt German bombers. Some models could carry two tons of bombs all the way to Berlin.

As an unarmed bomber, its speed and climbing ability outpaced the enemy. Some models could fly long distances, so they were used for reconnaissance. In all, 7,781 Mosquitos were built, including the 1,113 made in Canada.

During the war, de Havilland also built the Tiger Moth, a standard British trainer airplane. Before the Second World War, the company had built civilian aircraft: the Gypsy and Hornet Moths, Dragon, and Dragonfly. After the war, it built the first jet airliner, the Comet.

BRITISH AIRCRAFT PRODUCTION

In 1943, Great Britain employed 1,678,200 workers to produce 26,263 aircraft, roughly 17% of 151,761, the Allied total for the year. (The U.S. produced 57%, the British Commonwealth 3%, and the USSR 23%.)

British aircraft manufacturing was the responsibility of a special government ministry, the Ministry of Aircraft Production (MAP).

DODGING THE "BUZZ BOMB"

When Chapman returned to England in 1944, his handler ordered him to report to the Germans on the accuracy of the V-1 flying bombs—nicknamed "buzz bombs" because of the sound they made. The Germans were firing them from occupied France at London, and wanted to know exactly where the bombs were landing so they could adjust their aim. Actually, they were barely undershooting their targets, but Double Cross agents reported that they were overshooting. When the Germans adjusted their aim, they missed the city entirely.

the explosive in the coal store, Chapman handed it to the ship's captain.

On later missions, Chapman provided the Germans with secret documents doctored by Double Cross. Some included details about beaches close to where the actual Normandy invasion took place in June 1944, information Double Cross knew Hitler had already decided was false. Later, the crumbling German government praised Chapman for telling them the truth. The former crook had turned into a successful double agent and earned himself a prison pardon.

The V-1 flying bomb was a miniature unmanned airplane about 26 feet (8 m) long. It was powered by a primitive jet engine. Here one is seen in flight over London, England.

TOO GOOD TO BE TRUE

Albanian-born Elyesa Bazna wanted to be rich. He dreamed of being as wealthy as the foreigners he worked for, so in 1943, when he saw an easy way to make a lot of money, he went for it! He didn't care who won the war as long as he was well paid.

Up until the early 1940s, Bazna had worked as a servant for various diplomats connected to the American, German, British, and Yugoslavian embassies in Ankara, the capital of Turkey. Then, in 1942, he became the valet of the British ambassador to Turkey, Sir Hughe Knatchbull-Hugessen. The ambassador tended to do everyday tasks in the same way and at the same time each day, which made it easy for the faithful-appearing Bazna to sneak around—especially since the valet had the run of the residence when the ambassador wasn't home.

Knatchbull-Hugessen was careful about most things, but he did have one bad habit: he often carried home from the embassy a dispatch box of top secret documents to work on after hours. And, as Bazna noticed, the ambassador sometimes left the box alone in his study when he was bathing in the morning. One day Bazna quickly made a wax impression of the box's key. The ambassador never suspected. After some snooping, Bazna also found the combination to the residence safe. Now, when no one was looking, Bazna could read and photograph most of the top secret Allied documents flowing in and out of Ankara, some of which contained detailed plans of how the Allies intended to win the war.

It's easy to figure out who would pay big money for that knowledge! In October 1943, Bazna offered to sell the Germans two rolls of film for £20,000. At first, Ludwig Moyzisch, Bazna's contact at the German embassy, hesitated. He wasn't sure the photographed documents were real. But Moyzisch told German ambassador Franz von Papen about the film, and von Papen accepted the offer without even haggling over the cost. And paying Bazna in British currency presented no problem. After reading the documents, von Papen christened the new agent "Cicero," after the ancient Roman orator, because of the eloquence of his information. He was certain it was legitimate.

High-command officers in Berlin weren't so sure.

CENTERS OF INTRIGUE

During the Second World War, Portugal, Sweden, and Turkey were neutral nations that attracted agents from Axis and Allied countries trying to sway the neutrals to their cause. Both sides practiced shady business in the neutrals' capital cities (Lisbon, Stockholm, and Ankara) and there were many opportunities for espionage.

TURKEY 1943–44

Neutral Turkey was a center of intrigue and espionage caught between three giant powers: Germany, the Soviet Union, and the Western Allies. The British ambassador to Turkey tried to convince the Turks to enter the war to provide a base from which the Allies could mount a massive attack on Hitler's armies. The Turks refused because they were afraid they might be overrun by the German and Soviet armies.

Ministry of Foreign Affairs, Ankara, Turkey

Sir H. Knatchbull-Hugessen, British ambassador to Turkey, second from the right in the front row, at Ankara station

DIPLOMATIC IMMUNITY

Most nations send official representatives to live and work in other countries in order to help with the day-to-day affairs carried out between them. International agreements help diplomats do their work and also protect them. One agreement guarantees that an embassy belongs to the nation that occupies it and not to the host country. So, the British embassy in Turkey is Great Britain's sovereign territory—it does not belong to Turkey. This means that Turkish police have no authority there. Entering without permission would be like invading Great Britain itself.

Another agreement promises diplomatic immunity, which means (among other privileges) that a host government cannot arrest or try diplomats for any crimes committed there. This includes espionage, so embassies make perfect headquarters for spies.

Countries at war do not have embassies in each other's capitals, so lots of spying takes place on neutral territory where they do have embassies.

Occasionally the home country of a diplomat caught spying will waive (give up) diplomatic immunity, but it does not have to. A host nation can ask a government to recall a spy. If the government refuses to do so, the host nation can declare the spy *persona non grata* and expel the offender. The trouble is that the offending country might retaliate and also expel a spy.

Usually, host countries prefer not to admit they know who is spying! After all, the offending country would only replace the spy with another. It's safer and more efficient to follow the spies you know to see what they are up to.

RSHA

Two separate German groups collected foreign intelligence during the Second World War: Section VI of the Reich Security Main Office (also called RSHA) and the Abwehr. The RSHA was part of the Nazi party. The Abwehr was German military intelligence and part of the German government. For most of the Second World War, the RSHA and the Abwehr fought with each other over who would collect foreign intelligence.

Ludwig Moyzisch, Cicero's contact at the German embassy, was a member of the RSHA's Section VI.

OPERATION BERNHARD

Bazna was no fool when he asked to be paid in British pounds. In the 1940s the pound was international currency, accepted almost anywhere in the world. The Germans readily agreed to pay him in that currency because they had more of it than they could ever use—counterfeit pounds, created by skilled political and concentration camp prisoners. The forgery project was called Operation Bernhard after its chief, Major Bernhard Krüger.

Originally, the Germans planned to drop the counterfeit bills over England to cause economic instability. Instead, the Nazis used them to pay informants and foreign spies like Cicero or to buy weapons from resistance groups, who were often short of funds. The fake bills were also sold to unsuspecting buyers in neutral nations in exchange for real ones.

In total, the Germans produced about £140 million worth of counterfeit British currency, today worth about £3.5 billion or $5.25 billion U.S. After the war the British introduced new notes to prevent anyone from spending the German-made bills.

They wondered if the information had been planted to mislead them. Although a bombing raid on Bulgaria seemed to confirm that at least some of the documents were genuine, higher-ups remained suspicious. Cicero even provided documents that mentioned a top secret plan called Overlord (the code name for the Allied invasion of Europe). It all seemed too good to be true. But the Germans continued to purchase the photos for £15,000 a roll, and Bazna's fortune grew.

By December 1943, Bazna had amassed a good amount of cash. But the Allies now knew that something rotten was happening at the British embassy. A defector from the German embassy in Ankara brought news of Cicero. Who was this mysterious secret agent?

British agents investigated but could not identify Cicero. However, they did discover Knatchbull-Hugessen's habit of taking work home. A new alarm system was installed in the ambassador's residence so that Bazna had to carefully remove a fuse whenever he wanted to open the safe. But Knatchbull-Hugessen now brought less work home, so there was less to photograph. Bazna was not worried, because the Germans had already paid him £300,000—enough to live extravagantly in a South American villa overlooking the ocean with a beautiful mistress and servants to take care of him.

However, Bazna's retirement plans soon fell through when his South American bank discovered that his British currency was counterfeit. No wonder the Germans had never haggled over the price!

SPECIAL FORCES

THE MISSION SEEMS IMPOSSIBLE? CALL IN COMMANDOS!

Special forces—sometimes called commandos—are small, elite, well-trained units able to go places and execute assignments that larger, lesser-trained units couldn't accomplish. They must often infiltrate behind enemy lines, a very risky business indeed.

During the Second World War most commando units were made up of volunteers, good soldiers who were young, adventurous, and physically fit. Every commando learned specialized techniques like scaling mountains or igniting explosives, depending on which force he had joined. Many units were trained to use unusual equipment such as parachutes or manned torpedoes.

In addition, some commandos were trained to live off the land, just in case they were cut off from friendly troops. Many learned to cover their tracks, leaving no evidence behind. They often carried only the bare essentials, and even memorized geographical references instead of carrying maps. They knew how to hide and often traveled at night.

U.S. Marine Raiders, an elite group, 1944

Many missions were created to blow something up. Sometimes commandos were sent in to rescue people. In all cases the commandos tried to stay at least one step ahead of the enemy. They had to think fast on their feet.

Usually the first task was to enter a hostile environment unnoticed, using whatever resources the commandos could muster. Sometimes soldiers were recruited who spoke foreign languages fluently and knew the local customs well enough to blend in. In other cases commandos used parachutes to sneak behind enemy lines. Others made use of gliders, miniature submarines, amphibious vehicles, and even a river barge to move in close to their targets. But adventurous entrances were only the beginning—then the real danger began!

THE NETHERLANDS

The Netherlands is often called Holland. The people who live there call themselves Hollanders or Nederlanders, but people who live in English-speaking countries call them the Dutch.

BRANDENBURG REGIMENT

The Brandenburgers were Germans who had lived outside Germany and knew foreign languages and customs. It was an elite regiment of troops chosen because they could easily blend into the armies and civilian populations of Germany's neighbors. This regiment was filled with troops very different from the tall, blond, blue-eyed Nazi ideal that made up other elite German units.

By the middle of the Second World War many Brandenburgers had been assigned to companies made up of speakers of: Arabic, Czech, Dutch, English, Flemish, Polish, Russian, Romanian, Lithuanian, Latvian, Slovakian, and other languages.

Brandenburgers performed missions in nearly every theater of the war, from the desert in North Africa to the Russian front.

DIRTY TRICKS

A few pretenders play their parts so well that they go unnoticed—until it's too late. During the Second World War the German army had an entire regiment of great pretenders, the Brandenburg Regiment. (See Brandenburg Regiment, this page.) Brandenburgers looked, sounded, and acted like the locals of the area the Nazis were about to attack. But could they fool the Dutch, who might already suspect an invasion was coming?

After the Nazis occupied Poland in September 1939, they turned their attention to the countries west and north of Germany. In the spring of 1940, the Nazis took Denmark and Norway. The German army was on a roll, so Hitler prepared to execute Plan Yellow, the Nazi march on France. But first, two neutral nations stood in the way: Belgium and the Netherlands. (See The Netherlands, this page.)

For months, Germany readied its forces to advance into the Netherlands, but the weather was in control, not the Nazis. It was an unusually harsh winter. Often the temperatures were so low that engines wouldn't start. Some days, snow and heavy frosts made roads and runways slippery. Other days, heavy fog kept aircraft grounded. Time after time the attack was called off. British newspapers nicknamed this period the Phony War, but there was nothing phony about it; the Nazis were just waiting for the perfect moment.

Meanwhile, many Dutch weren't worried. They believed their country's neutrality protected them, and history did seem to be on their side. Germany hadn't invaded the Netherlands during the First World War, so the Dutch hoped the Nazis would leave them alone this time too. This was in spite of repeated warnings from the Dutch embassy in Berlin that the Germans were about to attack. Then a wake-up call rang loud and clear. Dutch intelligence discovered that Germans had smuggled Dutch army, police, and rail system uniforms into Germany.

Something was up, but what? Perhaps the Germans really did mean business. Just in case, the Dutch wired key bridges with demolition charges. If German troops approached the bridges, Dutch soldiers could blow the bridges to smithereens. That would slow the Germans down and give the Dutch time to gather their forces

DESTROYING BRIDGES

One way to slow down an enemy advance is to destroy bridges along their route. If a bridge that spans water is demolished, tanks and artillery can't cross until a temporary bridge is assembled, and infantry are forced to cross slowly, usually in small boats.

There are many reasons not to demolish a bridge in your own country during a war. For one, a blown-up bridge slows everyone down, not just the enemy. For another, every bridge that's destroyed must be rebuilt. Bridges are commonly rigged with explosives in wartime, but they are usually destroyed only when the enemy is about to take the bridge and there seems no hope of retaking it soon.

THE RULES OF WAR

The trick played by the Brandenburgers at Gennep might seem unfair or even dishonest, but it was legal according to the rules of war. These international agreements—part of The Hague Conventions and the Geneva Conventions—were signed by many of the world's nations before the Second World War.

According to the rules of war, wearing a disguise, such as an enemy uniform, can be a legitimate ruse. But if the disguised soldier is gathering information, he is a spy and can be executed. Actively participating in combat while in disguise is also illegal.

The rules of war restrict warring nations (called belligerents) from doing certain things. For example, it's illegal to use poison gas or to kill unarmed soldiers.

Countries don't always follow the rules of war. However, if a belligerent consistently violates the rules, injured nations might pay the belligerent back. And other countries could choose to help the injured nations punish the belligerent.

deeper inside the country to fight the Germans until Allied help arrived.

Unfortunately for the Dutch, the Germans knew about the wired bridges, so they developed their own scheme. It was a sneaky plan, requiring knowledge of foreign languages and customs—the kind of job the Brandenburg Regiment was good at.

One especially important bridge spanned the Maas River at Gennep, two miles (3.2 km) from the German border with the Netherlands. It was a railroad bridge, and its tracks headed into western Holland, right through the Dutch defensive line. If the Brandenburgers could save the bridge, two fully loaded troop trains would cross the border at H-hour—the start of the invasion.

When the German troops assembled near the border between Germany and the Netherlands, Brandenburger lieutenant Wilhelm Walther and his men dressed in civilian clothes and joined the crowds of frightened refugees fleeing the approaching army. No one noticed the Brandenburgers as they maneuvered through the throngs and headed towards Gennep. They were good at disguises, very good.

In the early morning hours on the day of the invasion, May 10, 1940, the Brandenburgers approached the eastern end of the railroad bridge. Two were dressed as Dutch military police and four were wearing raincoats. Although this was not an everyday occurrence, the guards at the bridge didn't shoot when they spotted them. After all, the police uniforms were authentic. Walther, who spoke Dutch fluently, phoned the western side of the bridge to say he was sending over four German prisoners of war (POWs). His story sounded OK, so the four in raincoats were handed over to genuine Dutch guards and then escorted to the hut on the opposite side. So far, so good. Still no one was suspicious.

Under armed guard, the four continued to act like POWs until they heard the rumble of the German troop trains. Suddenly the pretend POWs produced weapons from under their raincoats, revealing their German uniforms, and opened fire on their guards. Imagine the surprise and horror, especially of the sentry responsible

for setting off the explosives to demolish the bridge. Sentries weren't allowed to blow up bridges without special permission! (See Destroying Bridges, page 28.) What was he supposed to do now?

In the end, the Dutch sentry never got permission. The troop trains rolled through, the Netherlands was under siege, and the Brandenburgers chalked up another victory. Dirty trick or not, the German plot was brilliant.

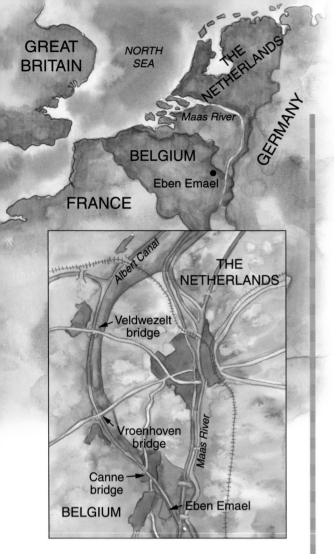

GREAT BRITAIN

NORTH SEA

THE NETHERLANDS

GERMANY

Maas River

BELGIUM

Eben Emael

FRANCE

Albert Canal

THE NETHERLANDS

Veldwezelt bridge

Vroenhoven bridge

Maas River

Canne bridge

BELGIUM

Eben Emael

Built into a Hill

Fort Eben-Emael had two main floors. Level 0, 150 feet (45 m) below the surface, contained barracks for 1,200 men. Level 1, 83.3 feet (25 m) below the surface, consisted of three miles (5 km) of tunnels connecting the command center, cupolas, and casemates.

The cupolas were reached from Level 1 by stairs that wound around the ammunition lifts. An elevator and two flights of stairs connected Level 1 to Level 0. Filters in the air system and airlock-like doors protected Level 0 from poison gas attacks. The stairs from Level 1 into the cupolas could also be sealed at the bottom.

> **GARRISON: troops who live in and guard a fort**

TERROR SWOOPED IN

Suspicious, unsure, fearful. This is how most of the world felt when Germany began rebuilding its military strength in the 1930s. The people of Belgium were particularly nervous, and for good reason! They shared a border with Germany. The Belgians figured that invading Nazis would cross three bridges spanning the Albert Canal, just 20 miles (32 km) from the German border. To protect themselves the Belgians developed a plan: they would destroy the bridges ahead of the intruders, and the 200-foot-wide (60-m-wide) canal with steep walls would force the bullies to find another route. This would buy time for Belgian reinforcements to come to the rescue.

Part of the plan was a fortress built at Eben-Emael—very modern for its time, and mostly underground. The fort had more than four miles (6.5 km) of passages that joined a command post, kitchens, hospitals, engine rooms, and barracks for 1,200 men. The underground area was so large that officers sometimes rode bicycles to get from one end to the other! Above-ground, an anti-tank ditch (a moat on three sides and the canal on the other) surrounded expanses of barbed wire, casemates, cupolas, minefields, and heavy artillery. The fort was invincible—or so the Belgians believed.

In fact, the modern fort didn't discourage the Nazis at all. The German military had a secret weapon, an amazing invention called a shaped charge. (See The Shaped Charge, page 31.) This was an explosive that, when detonated, could instantly penetrate armor plate with a tremendous blast of molten metal. As for getting to the fort, the Germans had done their homework. They decided to sneak into Belgium in gliders—planes with no engines, and thus very quiet. (See Gliders, page 33.) The fort's roof was perfect for landing, if only the pilots could learn to touch down in small spaces without crashing into each other.

For months, Group Granite (a special unit of glider pilots and engineers) practiced on wooden mock-ups of Eben-Emael that had been built using any information the Germans could get their hands on. Group Granite's eleven teams of seven or eight men were each assigned a different target. The pilots refined their landings, and each team practiced assembling shaped charges over and over. They never ignited them during practice, of course, since an explosion might give away their secret. (This operation was top secret. Security was tight.) Each man had to know his part in precise detail. All teams also had to be familiar with the others' targets, to help out in case things did not go according to plan.

Meanwhile, in 1939, quick as a flash, the Nazis invaded Poland. The attack was so sudden that it earned the name "lightning war," or *blitzkrieg* in German. By May 1940, Germany had also waged a blitzkrieg in Norway and Denmark. Europe was tense, wondering where the Nazis would attack next.

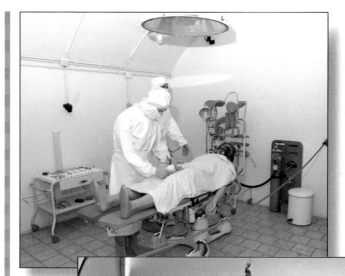

The surgery (left) and a non-commissioned officers' bedroom (below). Fort Eben-Emael is now a museum.

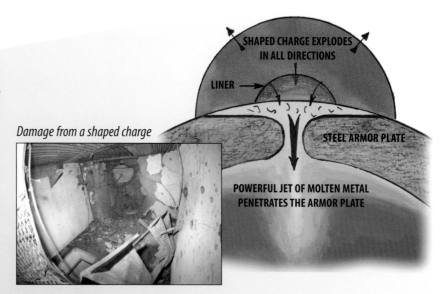

THE SHAPED CHARGE

A shaped charge is a thin metal cone or concave shape (called a liner) backed by an explosive, all of which is surrounded by a metal casing. When the explosive is detonated, the liner blasts forward at tremendous speed, creating a powerful jet of molten metal that can penetrate armor plate. It's important to position the shaped charge correctly. If it's placed too far from its target, the jet spreads and loses its power. If it's set at an angle, the jet bounces off.

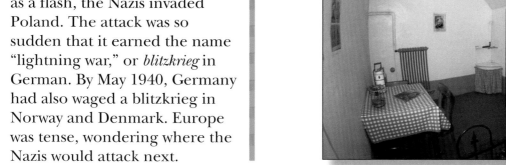

Damage from a shaped charge

SHAPED CHARGE EXPLODES IN ALL DIRECTIONS

LINER

STEEL ARMOR PLATE

POWERFUL JET OF MOLTEN METAL PENETRATES THE ARMOR PLATE

Eben-Emael's casemate walls were made of concrete 5 to 12 feet (1.5–3.5 m) thick, but it took only 20 minutes for the Germans to destroy them.

Cupola

Lightning was about to strike Belgium. A little after midnight on May 10, Eben-Emael was on alert: German troops had begun massing at the border. But since the invading troops were still 20 miles (32 km) away, the Belgians reacted slowly, totally unaware of … the surprise!

Just before dawn, 11 Ju-52s (see Ju-52, this page) took off from a German airport, each towing a glider. The mission was not without glitches, however: two gliders had to land in Germany. The tow rope connected to the glider carrying the unit commander snapped soon after takeoff. The second glider was released prematurely. (No wonder each team had to know every other team's business!) Leaderless at the German-Belgian border, nine gliders were released to descend into Belgium. Four hours later, unidentified objects were reported in the pre-dawn light. The Belgians had not a clue what these UFOs were! A short while later, dark silhouettes circled above Fort Eben-Emael and swooped onto their targets.

Well trained, the men of Group Granite easily subdued the Belgian garrison and knocked out nine of their targets within 20 minutes. First on the list were the casemates and their artillery, which would have been able to destroy the bridges over the Albert Canal. When the German commander finally arrived a few hours later—after commandeering another glider and tow—he found everything going according to plan. The months of practice had paid off.

Thirty-six hours after the gliders landed on Fort Eben-Emael, a trumpet announced the fort's surrender. German troops had taken two of the bridges undamaged; the third needed some repair. The door was open: the Nazis could sweep across Belgium and continue the blitzkrieg into France.

> **CASEMATE: *a reinforced enclosure in which artillery is mounted***

GLIDERS

In 1919, Great Britain, France, Italy, and the United States drew up the Treaty of Versailles to punish Germany for causing the First World War. Among other restrictions, the treaty prohibited Germany from having an air force. However, it didn't forbid the Germans from building and flying gliders, since gliders were aircraft without engines and therefore presumably non-military. The German government encouraged the formation of glider clubs to teach basic aviation skills.

When the Nazis came to power in 1933, glider pilots formed the core of the new German air force. Disobeying the Treaty of Versailles, the Nazis began building airplanes. But they realized they could also use gliders to transport troops. Gliders were silent, could land on nearly any flat surface, and in groups could land as a compact unit (unlike paratroopers, who tend to drift apart in the wind).

The gliders that landed at Eben-Emael carried eight men each. A much larger glider, the Me 321 Gigant, could carry 120 troops comfortably or 200 men in an emergency. The Gigant wasn't popular for two reasons. First, it needed a very powerful airplane to tow it. Second, fighter aircraft could easily shoot down a glider, and losing 200 men all at once was worse than losing 8.

Ju-52

The Ju-52 was a three-engine military transport plane built by the German firm Junkers. The first ones, built in the early 1930s, were airliners. After the Luftwaffe (the German air force) was created, Ju-52s were used briefly as bombers, then as transport planes to deliver the attacking forces and supplies during the invasions of Norway, Denmark, France, Belgium, and the Netherlands.

> **CUPOLA: *a rounded structure that houses a gun***

RIDING TORPEDOES

Durand de la Penne

HUMAN TORPEDOES

During the 1930s, Lieutenant Teseo Tesei of the Italian navy developed the slow-moving torpedo—officially called a *Siluro a lenta corsa*, which means "slow-course torpedo" in Italian. The name was often shortened to SLC. Unofficially, Italians called the SLC a pig because two commandos dressed in underwater diving gear rode on top of it—sort of like riding a real pig. An electric motor powered by batteries ran the propeller at the back, moving the pig through the water. Upon reaching the designated enemy ship, the commandos removed the head from the front of the pig and attached it to the target using magnets. The head contained explosives rigged out with a timing device to give the commandos time to get away. The Italians used pigs to sink ships in the British Mediterranean Fleet at Alexandria and Gibraltar.

Two Italian frogmen sat one behind the other on an odd-looking cigar-shaped vehicle. It was night. Lieutenant-Captain Durand de la Penne and his diving partner were submerged beneath the Mediterranean Sea, heading towards the harbor at Alexandria, Egypt—enemy waters. The strange vehicle was called a pig, an underwater machine that could maneuver through shallow water where submarines could not go. (See Human Torpedoes, this page.) Pigs were perfect for sneaking into harbors to commit sabotage. The frogmen's mission was to blow up the *Valiant*, a British warship anchored at Alexandria, the home of the British Mediterranean Fleet, which had been terrorizing convoys sailing between Italy and Libya, an Italian colony in North Africa.

On that same night in December 1941, two other teams under Durand de la Penne's command were also about to enter the harbor. Two miles (3.2 km) outside the harbor, the three Italian teams had left the submarine *Scirè*. Luck was with them as they passed undetected over minefields and an automatic warning system on the sea floor. Now they had to locate the narrow entrance through the breakwater, a barrier of rocks that reduced the force of waves on the ships anchored in the harbor. When they finally found the entranceway, they discovered it was blocked by three metallic anti-submarine nets, wired with explosives, and patrolled by marines. (See Submerged Metal Nets, this page.) What to do now? Suddenly, as if by magic, the nets opened. Actually, it wasn't at all supernatural: the British had just opened the nets to allow a convoy to enter.

Taking advantage of their luck, the Italians tailgated their way into the harbor and began looking for their targets. De la Penne found the *Valiant* easily but then suffered a stroke of bad luck: a steel cable entangled his pig's propeller. The pig stalled and sank. What's more, Durand de la Penne's partner seemed to have disappeared! The commander detached the pig's torpedo warhead and dragged it to beneath the *Valiant*. With enormous effort he tried desperately to attach the heavy explosive to the battleship's keel. But he just couldn't lift it high enough without help, so he had to leave it on the sea floor, where it would still do significant damage because the harbor was shallow.

Nearly exhausted, de la Penne searched for his partner and finally found him at the surface, clinging to a mooring buoy. He was still in a daze from falling off the pig when the propeller was damaged. Before they could reach shore and try to sneak back into Axis-held territory, the pair had more bad luck: sentries spotted and captured them. The Italian commandos refused to tell the British any more than their ranks and serial numbers, but the *Valiant*'s Captain Morgan thought he knew a way to scare the Italians into talking! He imprisoned them deep in the battleship, well below the ship's floating line, where they would most likely drown if something exploded and sank the ship. But the Italians remained silent.

Then, at 6 a.m., an explosion! A warhead planted by one of the other Italian commando teams detonated, damaging two other ships in the harbor: the tanker *Sagona* and the destroyer *Jervis*, which happened to be moored alongside the *Sagona* for refueling. Imagine the fear aboard the

SUBMERGED METAL NETS

Anti-submarine nets are underwater barriers made of steel wire that are stretched across the mouth of a harbor to keep out enemy submarines. Often attached to the nets are explosives that detonate when intruders run into them. Anti-torpedo nets, also made of wire, are positioned around ships at anchor to stop torpedoes from striking the hulls.

Italian frogmen used special gear filled with oxygen-rich air, breathing equipment originally designed for escaping from submarines. The system was sealed so no bubbles would rise to the surface to give the divers away. Technically, divers were restricted to shallow water, less than 45 feet (15 m) deep, but some divers did descend to 90 feet (30 m).

Queen Elizabeth–class Battleship (U.K.), c. 1941

CREW:
1,124 – 1,184 people

DIMENSIONS:
Length 643.75 feet (193.13 m)
Beam 104 feet (31.2 m)
Draft 30.66 feet (9.2 m)

ARMAMENT:
8 x 15-inch (381 mm) / 42 caliber Mk 1 guns (mounted in four twin turrets)
20 x 4.5-inch (113 mm) / 45 caliber QF guns (mounted in ten twin turrets)
Multiple 20 mm and 40 mm anti-aircraft (AA) guns

Valiant! At the last moment, de la Penne decided to talk. He sent Captain Morgan a message to warn him his ship too would soon blow up. This gave Morgan just enough time to evacuate his crew but not enough time to search for the explosives. A few minutes later the charge under the *Valiant* exploded, but the crew was safe.

A few minutes after that, a third charge went off under another battleship in the harbor, the *Queen Elizabeth*. (See Queen Elizabeth–class Battleship, page 36.) In all, six Italian commandos riding three modified torpedoes had crippled two of Britain's most powerful battleships as well as damaging a tanker and another destroyer. And the most amazing part: they had done it in the enemy's well-protected harbor.

However, because all six of the Italian commandos had been captured, no one reported the news to the Italian navy. Axis ships could now sail freely on the Mediterranean, but they didn't know it! It was not until months later that the Italian navy learned of the opportunity they had missed.

To make sure the Italian navy was fooled, the British created the illusion that the damaged ships were seaworthy, a trick that worked because the water in the harbor was only 15 to 50 feet (4.6–15 m) deep, and both battleships still had their upper decks well above water. For added realism, the funnels emitted smoke as if the ships were about to leave the harbor.

The six Italian commandos spent the rest of the Second World War as prisoners of war. After the war, they received the Italian Gold Medal for Military Valor. Durand de la Penne received his medal from Vice Admiral Charles Morgan, the former captain of the *Valiant* and now head of the Mediterranean Fleet.

Italian Gold Medal for Military Valor

HIDDEN AT GIBRALTAR

Although the attack at Alexandria in December 1941 was the most devastating episode involving pigs, the British Mediterranean Fleet was attacked more often at Gibraltar. This was because the Italians had a secret: the merchant ship *Olterra*. Of course, the British knew that the *Olterra* was interned across the bay from Gibraltar in neutral Spanish waters. Nothing looked suspicious. What the British didn't know about was hidden below the *Olterra's* waterline: a secret door. Pigs slipped out, planted explosives, and slipped back into the *Olterra* undetected—and the British never caught on.

COPYCAT PIGS

Impressed by the underwater sabotage committed by Italian commandos at Alexandria, the British developed the chariot, their version of the pig. The first mission involving chariots failed miserably. In November 1942, two chariots on their way to destroy a German warship in a Norwegian fjord broke free from the boat towing them and were lost in rough seas 10 miles (16 km) from where they were supposed to be launched. Later operations were more successful but also had problems. One chariot crashed into a merchant ship, another was damaged at launching, and the Germans captured many crews. But in October 1944 the last chariot attack of the war went very well: two teams based in the Far East sneaked into a Malay port, placed explosives on enemy ships, and then returned safely to their home submarine to watch the targets explode.

ITALY

Gran Sasso

Rome

SICILY

After the war, Lieutenant Colonel Otto Skorzeny waits to testify at a Nuremberg trial about war crimes.

PUPPET STATE: a country whose government is being controlled by the government of another country, much as a puppeteer controls the strings on a marionette

NAZI DAREDEVIL

O tto "Scarface" Skorzeny enjoyed taking risks. In fact, he had a flair for performing well in dangerous situations, and earned the name "the most dangerous man in Europe" as an SS officer. (See Schutzstaffel, page 39.) He commanded some of Germany's most daring special operations, but even a winner loses sometimes.

The scar on Skorzeny's left cheek was a gash carved from ear to chin during a sword duel when he was a university student in the late 1920s. A little more than a decade later he made a convincing mark on the world. His first big chance came when Hitler asked him to rescue Benito Mussolini, who had recently been forced from office as Italy's prime minister. (See Benito Mussolini, page 40.)

In 1943, the Allies invaded Sicily, a large island off Italy's southwest coast. Mussolini had joined Hitler in his quest for power, but now most Italians were tired of the war. So, when it looked like the Allies were going to invade mainland Italy, the Italian king replaced Mussolini with Pietro Badoglio, who was more willing to compromise with the Allies.

By September, Mussolini was under house arrest at a secluded ski resort 6,500 feet (1,980 m) above sea level, an isolated hideaway chosen to discourage rescue attempts. The only way to reach the resort was by cable railway or with parachutes or gliders. A surprise attack using the cable railway was not an option: Italian troops guarded the railway station at the bottom as well as the hotel at the top. And a parachute approach was too dangerous: at such a high altitude, the paratroopers might drop too quickly through the thin air, breaking legs and arms when they hit the ground. Besides, landing as a compact group ready for action would be difficult on the mountain's rocky terrain. Instead, Skorzeny and high-ranking officers of the parachute corps chose to use gliders. Even this was dangerous, because the only spot to land was a small triangular meadow behind the resort. Talk about difficult choices!

On the day of the assault, a battalion of paratroopers secured the cable railway to prevent Italian reinforcements from interfering with the rescue. Meanwhile, Skorzeny and his troops prepared to land in eight

ADOLF HITLER

Warped, egocentric, and willful, Adolf Hitler was one of the cruelest conquerors the world has ever known. He had a genius for making speeches, creating propaganda, and manipulating people, skills he used to become Germany's leader in 1933.

Hitler had joined the German Workers' Party in 1919. It was a group that claimed Germans were superior to all other nationalities. According to them, the government had given away their country's greatness—land and the right to build a military—when they signed the Treaty of Versailles at the end of the First World War.

Two years later, Hitler was the party's leader. He changed the party's name to National Socialist German Workers' Party, or Nazi for short. Hitler's speeches inspired crowds of unemployed and hungry Germans to join his party. By 1933, Hitler had transformed it into the election-winning Nazi party that believed in strong, centralized government headed by a leader with absolute power. Hitler used propaganda and terror to maintain his power, insisting that his dictatorship was the only way to save Germany from people he considered undesirable, such as Communists, Jews, Gypsies, homosexuals, and handicapped men, women, and children. During the course of the war, death camps were built and millions were murdered.

Immediately after assuming power, Hitler began building Germany's military. He then embarked on an aggressive campaign to expand Germany itself.

In 1938, German forces occupied Austria and made it a part of Germany. The same year, Hitler forced Czechoslovakia to hand over land settled by Germans, later conquering the entire country. The next year, his armies invaded Poland after faking Polish attacks on German territory.

It was becoming clear that Hitler wanted most of Europe. As Germany invaded country after country, Hitler grew more powerful at home. By 1941, Hitler had become the head of the German military, and he directed the strategy on each of Germany's fronts. Later in the war, some Germans knew that Hitler was evil, and others believed his actions would destroy Germany, so there were attempts on his life. Unfortunately, every attempt failed. In April 1945, with his empire crumbling, Hitler committed suicide.

Adolf Hitler poses with a group of SS members in Germany in 1933.

SCHUTZSTAFFEL

SS is short for Schutzstaffel, which in German means "protective squad." Originally, members of the SS were Hitler's personal guards, but by 1933 the SS had evolved into an elite group. Members of the SS were so blindly devoted to Nazi principles that they would go to almost any lengths to preserve them, including forcing foreigners into slave labor, trying to Germanize citizens of conquered territories, and murdering Jews, Gypsies, and Communists in concentration camps. Always a group separate from the regular German armed forces, towards the end of the war the SS controlled German intelligence as well as local police departments.

Mussolini and Hitler in Germany, 1940

BENITO MUSSOLINI

Benito Mussolini (also known as Il Duce, which means "The Leader" in Italian) was the leader of the Italian Fascist Party from 1919 to 1945. He was head of the Italian government from 1922 to 1943, rising to power through a mixture of political maneuvers and violence. Once in charge, he quickly extended the power of his government, making himself a dictator in everything but name. His dream was to build an Italian empire with the Mediterranean Sea as an "Italian lake." In 1935, he invaded and conquered Ethiopia, in northeast Africa. This aggression and his use of poison gas in the attacks were condemned by the League of Nations, a pre–Second World War organization created to maintain world peace. After his rescue by Skorzeny, Mussolini headed Hitler's puppet state (see Puppet State, page 38) in northern Italy until the end of the war, when Italian Communists killed him.

FIESELER FI-156 STORCH

The Storch was a German twin-engine aircraft built to carry only its pilot and one passenger. It was a light plane that could take off in less than 200 feet (60 m) and stop within 50 feet (15 m) of touchdown at sea level. As with all airplanes, the Storch needed a longer runway at higher altitudes to lift off and land.

gliders on the mountaintop target. But wait! The Alpine meadow was actually a steep, rocky hill that ended in a cliff! Aerial photography is hard to interpret.

A quick change of plans. One by one the gliders crashed into the rugged ground in front of the resort instead. Many of the gliders were now a mess of torn canvas and splintered wood. Skorzeny's glider, however, landed just 15 or 20 yards (14–18 m) from the hotel. He quickly ran up the incline, kicked the chair out from under a radio operator, and smashed the transmitter. Spotting Mussolini standing at a window, he ran up a flight of stairs three at a time and threw open the door to his room. Within four minutes Skorzeny and his men had subdued all resistance and he was by Mussolini's side.

But Skorzeny's problems weren't over. He still had to figure out how to get Mussolini off the mountain. Plan A, to descend the cable railway then escape in a twin-engine Heinkel from a captured airfield nearby, was scrapped because the German radio operator couldn't reach his contact to call the plane up from Rome. Plan B, to descend the cable railway then take off in a lighter plane from the valley, was abandoned because that plane's landing gear had been badly damaged on landing. Plan C was risky and involved the Storch reconnaissance aircraft that was flying overhead just in case the first two plans failed. (See Fieseler FI-156 Storch, this page.) Although the pilot skillfully landed the Storch on a hastily cleared "runway" close to the hotel, he was worried the plane might not take off again: the runway was short and planes at high altitudes need a long run to take off. To make matters worse, Mussolini was a big man with heavy baggage, so the plane needed an even longer runway. As if this wasn't enough, Skorzeny insisted on boarding the Storch too.

Afraid that he was about to crash to his grave, the pilot opened the throttle wide while 12 men gripped the wings to hold the plane back, allowing it to gather as much force as possible before heading down the runway. When he signaled for the men to let go, the plane surged forward and finally took off … and then came down again, hitting a rock! The plane toppled

DFS 230

The main German troop-carrying glider was the DFS 230. DFS 230A-1s were used to capture the fortress Eben-Emael (see Terror Swooped In, page 30) and DFS 230C-1s (a later model with braking rockets to reduce landing distance) were used to rescue Mussolini.

DFS 230A-1

Crew:
    2 pilots + 8 passengers
Engine:
    none
Weight: 1,896 lb. (860 kg) empty, 4,630 lb.
    (2,100 kg) with maximum load
Dimensions: 37' x 9', 68.75' wingspan
    (12.2 x 2.7 m, 20.9 m wingspan)
Armament:
    none

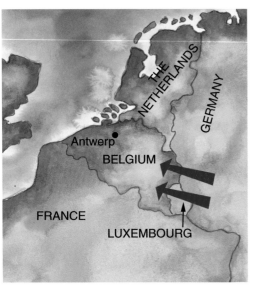

In December 1944, German forces counterattacked the American army in an attempt to re-enter Belgium. Skorzeny's units were part of this last major offensive.

PANZER: the short form of the German word for tank, *panzer-kampfwagen,* **which means "armored fighting vehicle".**

over the edge of the cliff into a dive.

For a few frightening moments the plane plunged towards the ground. Then a miracle! The pilot gained control and Mussolini's rescue was a success.

Later, the paratroopers on top of the mountain descended to the valley by the cable railway, then returned to their base in trucks.

Skorzeny was awarded the Knight's Cross, and although the parachute corps had participated significantly in the operation, Skorzeny became known as the hero and was featured in German newsreels and radio broadcasts. Skorzeny proved himself a winner many more times, successfully completing daring operations in eastern Europe. But near the end of the war his luck changed.

When Hitler was preparing his last major offensive on the Western Front in December 1944, he called on Skorzeny to lead another special operation, code-named Panzer Brigade 150—a name designed to trick the enemy into thinking it was a tank brigade rather than a special forces unit. Part of Skorzeny's unit was to get behind Allied lines by pretending to be retreating American tanks. Once there, they would be able to create chaos among the Allies. But Panzer Brigade 150 faced problems from the very beginning. Instead of the 15 captured U.S. tanks that Skorzeny requested, he got five German ones. This meant his unit had to modify the vehicles to look like U.S. tanks. The job was so poorly done that Skorzeny believed the altered tanks would only fool inexperienced troops at night and from a long way away. As it turned out, the bad job didn't matter. On the morning of the operation, the altered tanks were snarled up in traffic. They ended up behind other German units and never reached the Allied lines at all!

The rest of Skorzeny's unit fared only a little better. Wearing American uniforms and carrying false identification, nine teams managed to sneak through Allied lines. Although they created little physical damage, they did cause unease and distrust—sentries began to stop any American soldier they didn't recognize and quiz him with trivia, such as the latest baseball standings and newest music hits. Such a faint victory for Skorzeny, a soldier accustomed to awesome triumphs.

OUTFOXING THE DESERT FOX

Second Lieutenant David Stirling felt frustrated. It was the spring of 1941 and the British were losing ground in North Africa. (See The Desert War 1941–42, this page.) General Rommel (the Desert Fox) and his elite Afrika Korps had outmaneuvered them at almost every turn. Although Stirling's commando unit had tried three times to disrupt German communications and interrupt supply lines in Libya, each mission had failed. Although he was only a junior officer, Stirling was sure he knew a way for the British to outsmart the Germans, but his idea still needed work. Basically, his concept was to take the Germans by surprise by smuggling teams of four or five highly trained soldiers behind the German lines where they could destroy aircraft, cut off communications, and create confusion while other British troops carried out a major offensive.

Jock Lewes, an officer in the Welsh Guards, agreed with Stirling that his idea would give British troops the advantage they needed. Lewes scrounged some parachutes, thinking that one way to sneak commandos behind enemy lines would be to drop them in after dark. Stirling—always up for an adventure—practiced dropping from an old Vickers Valentia. (See Risky Business, page 44.) Unfortunately, his parachute snagged on the aircraft's tail, tearing a hole in the chute's fabric. He fell way too fast! When he hit the ground, he injured his legs and

THE DESERT WAR 1941–42

At the beginning of the Second World War, Egypt was a British colony and Libya was Italian. The British and Italians fought in North Africa for control of the region. By early 1941, the British had gained ground in the Western Desert, as they then called North Africa. They had just about ejected the Italians from Libya when the Germans sent the Afrika Korps, commanded by Lieutenant General Erwin Rommel (the Desert Fox), to help the Italians. Even before Rommel's troops were up to full strength, the Afrika Korps mounted an offensive that completely surprised the British. Although the German troops were fewer in number and lacked needed supplies, Rommel was wily like a fox, and his troops inflicted heavy losses on the British. But when it looked like the Desert Fox was going to overrun Egypt, in July 1942, the seesaw tilted again. By then the Germans had only a few dozen tanks and their supplies were low. The British, with more soldiers and supplies, were soon in control, forcing the Germans to retreat. By early 1943, the Afrika Korps had completely withdrawn from Libya.

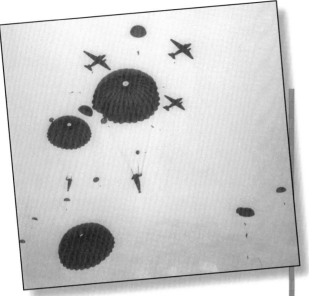

WWII parachutists

RISKY BUSINESS

When David Stirling used a Vickers Valentia to practice parachute jumping, he was flirting with danger. The Valentia was a twin-engine biplane built in the early 1930s for transporting passengers, so it lacked the rail to which static lines were normally hooked. Paratroopers didn't open their own chutes in those days. The static line jerked the parachute open when the paratrooper fell to the length of the line, ensuring that he was a safe distance below the plane. Because the Valentia didn't have a rail, Stirling tied the static line to a seat in the plane.

> **BRIGADE: *an army unit of 3,000 to 7,000 men, usually divided into three battalions***

LEWES BOMB

Jock Lewes developed the Lewes bomb when he was challenged to come up with an explosive that was small enough to carry yet powerful enough to destroy aircraft. The bomb was made of oil and thermite, a substance that can burn through most metals. Each Lewes bomb weighed only one pound (0.5 kg), so one man could carry enough to wipe out a whole squadron of planes.

back, and had to spend two months recuperating in a hospital—plenty of time to develop his small-group commando theory further.

Upon his release, Stirling decided to deliver his idea in person to Commander-in-Chief General Auchinleck in Cairo. He knew he was supposed to go through proper channels, but he was afraid the general would never see his theory if he followed British military protocol. His first hurdle was to get past the guard, since he couldn't enter headquarters without a pass. Bluffing didn't work, so he squeezed through a gap in some barbed wire fencing, which was tricky because he was still on crutches and had to leave them behind, leaning against a tree. While a staff car distracted the guard, Stirling slipped into the building, then ducked into an office. Bad choice! The office belonged to a major who remembered Stirling as a student who'd slept through his lectures. There was no help there!

Luckily, the next office he entered was friendlier. It belonged to the deputy commander, General Neil Ritchie, who was willing to listen as Stirling pitched his theory. Impressed, Ritchie agreed to pass the idea on to the commander-in-chief. As it turned out, General Auchinleck liked it too! Three days later, Stirling was promoted to captain and instructed to select teams from the remains of his recently disbanded commando brigade. Stirling's new unit was called L Detachment, Special Air Service Brigade (also known as SAS). The name was chosen to fool German intelligence into thinking the British had formed a whole new airborne brigade.

Although Ritchie and Auchinleck were willing to give Stirling's idea a go, in the beginning not everyone was convinced the idea would work. One Royal Air Force (RAF) group captain declared it would be impossible to raid a German airfield. But Stirling was positive his plan was sound, so he bet £10 that he could. To prove it, he raided the main RAF air base near Cairo and placed labels on planes to show where he could have planted bombs!

Proving his theory would work suited Stirling's sense of adventure. However, waiting weeks for official parachuting instructions to arrive from England did not, so

some of the initial SAS lessons included innovative techniques such as how to land by rolling backwards out of a truck traveling 30 miles per hour (48 k.p.h.). As you might expect, a few trainees broke some bones! But in spite of the training hazards, the SAS was ready for the first scheduled raid.

Stirling organized the SAS into small units, each of which was to parachute close to an enemy airfield, plant delayed-action explosives developed by Jock Lewes, then walk to a rendezvous point to be picked up by trucks driven by LRDG patrols. (See LRDG, this page.) The night of November 17 was very windy, but morale was high, so Stirling decided to jump in spite of the weather. Later he realized that he should have waited: many of the troops landed in a blinding sandstorm far from their targets, and only 22 of 66 commandos survived. Stirling was among those who did get back.

David Lloyd Owen of the LRDG helped turn the SAS's fortunes around. Since the parachute idea had been a failure, Owen suggested that his men drive the SAS to future missions. This was a great idea because LRDG trucks could move quickly across the desert, traveling deeper inland than the enemy lines, which pretty much hugged the Mediterranean shoreline. The truck drivers could drop men within a few miles of their targets and later transport them back.

About a year later, after many successful operations in Libya using vehicles, the British finally forced the Desert Fox to retreat into Tunisia. The SAS continued to harass the Germans as they moved west, but the flat desert changed into a hilly land of scrubby shrubs, which slowed down the vehicles. Many members of the SAS were captured in Tunisia, including Stirling in 1943. Although Stirling spent most of the rest of the Second World War as a prisoner, the SAS continued to operate in Italy, France, and Germany until the end of the war.

LRDG

The Long-Range Desert Group (LRDG) was a volunteer unit created in 1940. The LRDG specialized in reconnaissance covering expanses of desert that only Arabs dared to cross. Sometimes the unit stayed out on secret patrols for weeks. The group traced its origins back to the Light Car Patrols of the First World War, who pioneered the art of desert driving in Model T Fords. During the Second World War, the LRDG used modified trucks.

SAS

From its creation, the Special Air Service had been an informal "beg, borrow, steal, or otherwise possess" organization, but by January 1943 it had been placed on a formal footing. The 1st SAS was composed of 5 squadrons, each with 10 officers and 90 enlisted men (called "other ranks" in British parlance).

TRY, TRY AGAIN

The race was on! Both the Allies and the Axis were eager to get their hands on a hard-to-get but necessary ingredient: heavy water. (See Heavy Water, page 50.) And both wanted to prevent the other from getting it, because whoever made the first atomic bomb would likely win the Second World War.

When the German army invaded Norway in 1940, the Nazis got much more than a long coastline from which to launch submarines to terrorize the North Atlantic. They also gained the Norsk Hydro fertilizer plant at Rjukan, which made heavy water. Of course, the Allies wanted to destroy the factory—but how? The fertilizer factory was perched on a rock shelf, part of a deep gorge with steep cliffs overlooking a peaceful valley 75 miles (120 km) west of Oslo. And it was well protected by a minefield, a barbed wire fence, machine-gun posts, and plenty of guards.

In October 1942, four British-trained Norwegians—members of the Norwegian resistance and originally from the area—dropped in by parachute to scout out the heavy-water plant. They radioed the British their findings, and a month later about 30 commandos tried to sneak into Norway in two Horsa gliders, each towed by a Halifax bomber. (See Halifax Bomber, page 48.) They were supposed to be guided by the four resistance fighters who had parachuted in a month earlier, but it was too cloudy and the pilots decided to turn back, 30 miles (48 km) from the drop zone. One bomber smashed into a hill, taking its glider with it. The tow rope on the other snapped, so its glider suddenly fell into Nazi-held territory. Only one Halifax bomber got back to Great Britain; the rest of the commandos died in Norway. Some were killed in the crash and some died later from their injuries. Still others were captured then executed by German troops, in violation of the rules of war.

Team Sparrow, as the four Norwegian resistance fighters were called, survived for three harsh winter months by eating reindeer meat and making pudding of the brains, blood, and flour. They also drank reindeer blood for needed vitamins and boiled the contents of the animals' stomachs.

At the end of February, the British tried sabotaging

AIRSPEED HORSA

The British troops flew into Norway in Airspeed Horsa gliders, each one carrying 15 commandos. Because Horsas were constructed almost entirely of wood, they were made by furniture companies instead of the overstretched aircraft industry.

NORWEGIAN RESISTANCE

During the Second World War, almost every occupied country had a resistance movement. When the German army invaded Norway in 1940, many Norwegians tried to undermine the enemy using sabotage, espionage, general disruption, and protest. They also established an underground printing press and helped persecuted groups and captured military personnel escape to safer territories. British intelligence easily found agents and contacts in Norway to work for the Allied cause.

A Halifax bomber similar to the two that towed the Horsa gliders over Norway in 1942

HALIFAX BOMBER

The Halifax bomber was a four-engine heavy bomber manufactured from 1940 to 1946 by Handley Page, a British company. It became one of the best combat planes of the Second World War when later models were improved by the installation of a third gun turret, more powerful engines, and better flight stabilizers. Although the Halifax was primarily a bomber, it was also used to hunt U-boats, drop paratroops and supplies, ferry troops, and tow gliders.

SOE

The Special Operations Executive was created as part of the Ministry of Economic Warfare in 1940. It was a combination of organizations that had previously belonged to the British army and the Secret Intelligence Service. SOE was led by its director, code-named CD. It was organized into headquarters sections and country sections.

HEADQUARTERS SECTIONS INCLUDED:
Clandestine Communications, Air, Naval, Security, and Liquidation (Mediterranean)— a sinister-sounding group whose job was to dispose of fishing boats SOE had used.

COUNTRY SECTIONS INCLUDED:
DF (responsible for escape routes) , X (responsible for operations in Germany), N (responsible for operations in the Netherlands), and others.

Many female SOE agents came from the First Aid Nursing Yeomanry (FANY), which they then continued to use as a cover occupation.

the heavy-water plant again. This time, six more British-trained Norwegians parachuted into Norway, 30 miles (48 km) from their target, and walked straight into a blizzard before joining up with Team Sparrow as planned. Guns and explosives on their backs, the commandos climbed down the treacherous cliffs on the opposite wall of the gorge, then approached the plant from below. This route was unguarded because the Germans had assumed the gorge was too steep for an attack. After cutting their way through the barbed wire fence surrounding the factory, the commandos crept in and placed their bombs. They also scattered British paratroop badges to make sure the Germans knew who was responsible—they didn't want the Nazis to blame the locals. They then escaped without having to fire a single shot. One group, armed and in uniform, skied 300 miles (480 km) to neutral Sweden. The rest spread out and hid, while German soldiers looked high and low for them but didn't catch a single one!

Because the plant was quickly repaired, the resistance fighters had stalled the production of heavy water for only half a year. The Americans were so concerned about the factory that they made the third attempt to destroy it. In November 1943, 143 American bombers dropped more than 700 bombs on it. The plant was damaged, innocent lives were lost … and the heavy-water equipment survived!

But the Germans had had enough. Word leaked out that they planned to ship the existing heavy water and all production equipment to Germany, because this would be easier than building their own plant. On February 20, 1944, members of the Norwegian resistance sneaked aboard the ferry that was about to haul the equipment and barrels of heavy water across Lake Tinnsjo on its way to Germany. Norwegian resistance fighters placed a bomb on board, timed to blow up when the ferry was in the middle of the lake, at its deepest part. The target sank in 1,500 feet (460 m) of water. Finally, the Allies had stopped the Nazis from obtaining a critical ingredient for manufacturing an atomic bomb.

Left, the mushroom cloud from an atomic bomb, Nagasaki, Japan, August 8, 1945

Below, the atomic bomb named Fat Man

MANHATTAN PROJECT

Scientists in Los Alamos, New Mexico, produced three atomic bombs in 1945 using uranium and a man-made material called plutonium. One bomb was successfully tested in New Mexico in July. Another—known as Little Boy—was dropped on Hiroshima, Japan, on August 6. Three days later, because the Japanese had not surrendered, the Americans dropped the third bomb—Fat Man—on Nagasaki. The atomic bombs caused incredible destruction and horror, and brought the war to a close. Some say the atomic bombs saved more lives over the long run than they destroyed, because the war was dragging on with many casualties. One of the tragedies of war is that innocent people are killed.

HEAVY WATER

Heavy water tastes like regular water. It looks like regular water. In fact, it's in the water we drink . . . and most of us don't know it's there! Water and heavy water are practically twins: the difference is so tiny you can't see it even under a microscope. Each molecule of water—the smallest amount of water you can possibly have—is made of two hydrogen atoms and one oxygen atom. Each molecule of heavy water is made of two deuterium atoms and one oxygen atom. Deuterium is hydrogen with something extra: a neutron, which makes it a teeny bit heavier.

At the beginning of the Second World War, German scientists believed they needed heavy water to develop an atomic bomb. Although it's every-where, there isn't very much. The only company that was making it in large quantities was Norsk Hydro, which explains why the Allies and Axis were so interested in that fertilizer factory.

OVER AND OUT

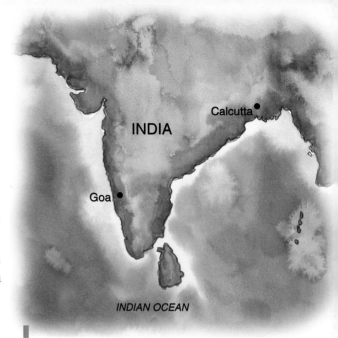

Yes, the mission was illegal, but the British believed it was absolutely necessary. In early 1943, German torpedoes had sunk a number of Allied merchant ships on the Indian Ocean. The Nazis seemed to have inside knowledge about ship courses and cargoes. Someone was sending German submarines secret information—but who?

A spy ring! Four Axis merchant ships were docked in the main harbor of Goa, a neutral Portuguese colony on the western coast of India. Radio direction-finding equipment revealed that one of them, the German *Ehrenffehls*, was illegally transmitting messages. But discovering the culprit was the easy part; how to destroy the transmitter without getting caught was a harder problem. The *Ehrenffehls* was safe in neutral territory, and the British couldn't legally touch her as long as she stayed there. To make matters even more complicated, the British didn't want to anger the Portuguese. Portugal might then refuse to let the Allies land aircraft in the Azores, Portuguese islands in the Atlantic Ocean about halfway between North America and Europe.

So, instead of attacking the *Ehrenffehls*, the British first tried bribery. But it didn't work—the ship's captain refused to sail out of Portuguese waters. The British next kidnapped the spymaster, who had been giving instructions to the spies from aboard the *Ehrenffehls*. (See spymaster, page 53.) This trick didn't work either: German torpedoes continued to sink Allied ships.

Fortunately, Colonel Lewis Pugh, a member of the Special Operations Executive (SOE), had another idea. (See SOE, page 48.) Pugh had friends in the Calcutta Light Horse, an auxiliary cavalry regiment on the northeastern coast of India. True, the members of the Calcutta Light Horse were mostly middle-aged businessmen on weekdays and soldiers only on weekends—it was more of a sporting and gentleman's club than a military unit—but that was an ideal cover. If caught, the raiders could claim to be cronies who had planned the operation while socializing in their club's bar. On the other hand, if regular troops were apprehended, the raid would look official and British relations with Portugal would definitely be strained.

THE LAWS OF NEUTRALITY

The Laws of Neutrality are supposed to protect nations that are not at war. All nations who have signed the laws—included in The Hague Conventions and the Geneva Conventions—are expected to obey them.

According to the Laws of Neutrality, countries at war (called belligerents) cannot send troops or military supplies across a country that is not at war (called a neutral). Also, belligerents cannot enter neutral sea or airspace.

If belligerent troops and property enter neutral territory, they must be interned (stay there). They cannot take further part in the war. Even troops fleeing into neutral territory to avoid capture, or a belligerent warship that stays in a neutral port for 24 hours, must be interned.

Individual citizens of a neutral state can voluntarily join the army of a belligerent, but organized groups of volunteers may not form in neutral territory.

A neutral cannot provide military supplies to a nation at war, but a belligerent can buy material from a company in a neutral state.

A neutral state must prevent belligerents from shipping military material across its territory, but it is not obliged to stop shipments made by private individuals.

If the Laws of Neutrality are broken, a neutral country can respond with force.

Fifteen members of the Calcutta Light Horse accepted the challenge. Pugh sent them by rail across India to a port closer to Goa. At the same time, Pugh and two other SOE agents navigated a barge from Calcutta to Goa. What kind of official operation would sail the high seas halfway around India on a clumsy flat-bottomed riverboat? A mission that needed a sailing vessel right away— a good boat was hard to find. And the barge would look harmless entering Goa's harbor.

Meanwhile, other members of the Calcutta Light Horse were doing their part to help the cause. One trooper bribed Goan officials to hold a party on the night of the planned raid. Of course, the captains of the four Axis ships were invited. The trooper also arranged for a carnival to be held in Goa on the same night, to lure the regular sailors off their ships.

According to plan, only a few members of the *Ehrenffehls* crew were aboard when the middle-aged marauders arrived alongside the hull. Using grappling hooks and ladders, spry members of the Calcutta Light Horse scaled the ship's sides and easily secured the bridge and engine room. But wait! The tiny crew left on board, not wanting their ship to fall into enemy hands, began setting it afire. Such confusion! Chaos! The raiders had to quickly search high and low to find the transmitter. Finally, they found it behind a closed door in the engine room. At last, the transmitter was smashed and over and out forever. Allied merchant ships were safe on the Indian Ocean again.

To all but a few, the identity of the raiders remained a mystery for 30 years … although there were rumors. Shrewd Allies spread the story that Nazi and anti-Nazi crew aboard the ship had caused the fighting and damage. No one could prove otherwise, so the operation had to be considered a British triumph … except for one unexpected turn of events. When one of the raiders returned to Calcutta, his business partner told him some bad news: their firm had insured the ships for £4.5 million. Oops!

WWII NEUTRAL NATIONS

Neutrals during the Second World War included Portugal, Spain, Switzerland, and Sweden. Norway, Holland, and Belgium were neutral until the Germans attacked them.

> **SPYMASTER: someone who gives orders to, and receives information from, spies**

German U-boat (submarine), 1939

Type VII U-boat

The Type VII was a common seagoing submarine. Seven hundred of various types were produced.

Type VIIC
Crew: 44
Dimensions: 218' x 20' x 16' (66.5 m x 6.2 m x 4.75 m)
Maximum speed (surfaced): 20.1 m.p.h. (32.4 k.p.h.)
Maximum speed (submerged): 8.6 m.p.h. (13.9 k.p.h.)
Armament:
1 x 88 mm gun
1 x 37 mm Anti-Aircraft (AA) gun
2 – 8 x 20 mm Anti-Aircraft (AA) guns
5 x 533 mm torpedo tubes (4 forward, 1 aft)

> **U-BOAT: German submarine (short for Unterseeboot, which means "undersea boat")**

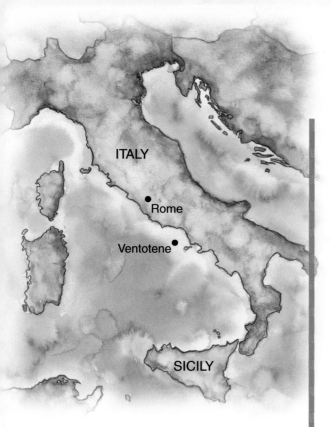

ITALY

Rome

Ventotene

SICILY

WAR-WEARY

Tired, defeated, and disillusioned ... by mid-July 1943 many Italians were fed up with the war. The Allies had recently pushed the Axis out of Italy's North African colonies, so dreams of an Italian empire were dashed. Even worse, many Italian soldiers were dead or wounded. From the very beginning, equipment used by the Italian army had been inferior to that of the Germans and Allies. And ammunition and other supplies had been inadequate for months. Some wondered why Italy had entered the war in the first place!

Even government and military higher-ups wanted to break the pact that Mussolini had signed with Hitler in 1939. (See Benito Mussolini, page 40, and Adolf Hitler, page 39.) But Mussolini had not yet faced the reality of his country's grim situation. He didn't seem to know that he was the most hated man in Italy and that a conspiracy to overthrow him had been in the works for more than six months. Now that the Allies were defeating Italian soldiers on home soil—on the island of Sicily, off the toe of boot-shaped Italy—the conspirators were even more eager to get rid of Mussolini and end the fighting.

Continued on page 56

HOODWINKED

Italy's situation was tense ... very tense. It was the summer of 1943, and most Italians were tired of fighting. (See War-weary, this page.) For weeks, Prime Minister Badoglio had been bargaining for a ceasefire with the Allies, trying to get the best possible terms. He especially wanted to protect Rome, the country's capital, from a probable German invasion. He was afraid the Nazis would punish Italy for giving up. In fact, German soldiers were already scattered throughout the Italian peninsula because they had been fighting the Allies alongside the Italians. What if they now turned on their former partners?

Badoglio's talks with the Allies had taken so long that his worst nightmares were coming true. Hitler had heard rumors that the Italians were working out a truce, so he sent in five more infantry and two more tank divisions (about 100,000 soldiers). By early September, the Germans were closing in on Rome. Badoglio had been right—it would not be easy to break the 1939 agreement signed by former prime minister Mussolini.

Quick action was needed. Saving Rome required special troops—paratroopers. The Americans planned to drop the entire U.S. 82nd Airborne Division into the city. But first the Americans needed to destroy the German radar detachment on the island of Ventotene, 30 miles (48 km) southwest of Rome in the Gulf of Gaeta. (See Radar, page 57.) Otherwise the detachment's radar equipment would warn the Germans that the aircraft carrying the paratroopers were approaching. Paratroopers dropping out of the sky would be easy pickings for the German anti-aircraft artillery positioned all around Rome!

On September 8, the day before the intended airdrop, the 509th Parachute Battalion (part of the U.S. 82nd Airborne Division), led by Captain Charles W. Howland, made an amphibious landing on Ventotene. (They arrived by sea because the radar would detect any aircraft and falling paratroopers.) Soon the paratroopers happened upon a good omen—an elderly Italian college professor who had been exiled to the island by the Mussolini government. As it turned out, he not only was friendly towards the Americans but could speak perfect

Continued from page 54

The British, with limited American troop support, were planning to capture all of Italy and establish air bases from which to bomb Germany.

Then, on July 25, a surprise: Italy's King Victor Emmanuel replaced Mussolini with Marshal Badoglio. Almost immediately the new leader hinted that he wanted to surrender. Chalk one up for the Allies!

But hold on—pulling out of the war would not be that easy. Hitler would certainly punish the Italians for leaving the Axis partnership.

Unfortunately, negotiations dragged on and on, giving Hitler ample time to send in troops to occupy Italy. At last, on September 3, Badoglio signed a surrender agreement. As predicted, the Germans did punish Italy for surrendering to the Allies. Many Italian soldiers were captured and killed or sent to Germany as prisoners of war. On September 9, Badoglio and King Victor Emmanuel fled Rome. Instead of getting out of the war, Italy remained an occupied nation and battlefield until April 1945.

THE ALL-AMERICANS

During the First World War, the 82nd Airborne Division was nicknamed the All-American Division because the unit had troops from every state in the U.S.A.

U.S. ARMY RANKS

The officer ranks of the U.S. army were:

- ✪ General of the Army (highest)
- ✪ General
- ✪ Lieutenant General
- ✪ Major General
- ✪ Brigadier General
- ✪ Colonel
- ✪ Lieutenant Colonel
- ✪ Major
- ✪ Captain
- ✪ 1st Lieutenant
- ✪ 2nd Lieutenant (lowest)

English. What's more, he had befriended the commander of the German radar detachment and believed he could get him to surrender without a battle.

While the professor approached the German commander, Howland split his troops in two. One platoon guarded the foot of the hill on which the radar equipment was placed, in case the Germans chose to fight. The other platoon, headed by Lieutenant Kenneth R. Shaker, waited to accept the detachment's surrender. The professor negotiated for 20 minutes and then informed Shaker that the German commander—a major—would surrender only to an officer of equal or higher rank.

Now, the rank of lieutenant is lower than major … but Lieutenant Shaker was a quick thinker: he told the professor to tell the major he was a full colonel with an entire battalion of troops (roughly 1,000 men) ready to attack. The bluff worked. The major and his 114 men descended the hill unarmed, first destroying the radar to prevent it from falling into Allied hands. Imagine how upset the major was to discover that Shaker was only a lowly lieutenant. Hoodwinked! But at that point, what could the Germans do?

The men of the 509th had accomplished their mission with no lives lost—a victory to be proud of. But the reason they had captured the detachment—the scheduled raid on Rome by the 82nd Airborne—had been canceled. On the same day as the Ventotene raid, the Americans announced that the Italian government had accepted an unconditional surrender. German units had moved quickly to disarm all Italian troops, and the Germans had occupied most of Italy. If the 82nd Airborne had parachuted into Rome, the entire division would have been massacred.

German prisoners on their way to prison camp, Italy, February 1944

A Royal Air Force guard watches over German technicians who are putting together captured radar equipment to be sent to England for further research.

Wurzburg radar

RADAR

Radar—short for "radio detection and ranging" —is a system that sends out ultra-high-frequency radio waves in a beam. When the beam strikes an object, it is reflected back, causing blips of light to appear on a fluorescent screen that indicate, among other things, the direction and proximity of the object. During the Second World War, radar was used for land-based, airborne, and shipboard detection.

Before the war, the Americans, British, and Germans had simultaneously developed radar in secret. In 1939 the British system was the most advanced, so they shared it with the Americans. By 1940 the Germans too had good radar. Both sides continued to improve their radar systems throughout the war.

Two early radars used by the Germans were Freya and Wurzburg.

Freya was an early-warning set, capable of detecting aircraft at ranges of up to 75 miles (120 km), but incapable of determining their height. Its companion radar was the Wurzburg.

The Wurzburg could not detect aircraft more than 25 miles (40 km) away, but it could track them more precisely and determine altitude (so a gun could be aimed using the radar data). Together this pair was deployed all across occupied Europe.

Later the Germans introduced a variety of other radars, including the Mammut (a very large early-warning radar), Seektat (a naval gunnery radar), and Lichtenstein (an airborne radar).

ITALY

Rome

Anzio

THE BLACK DEVILS

The fighting at Anzio, Italy, was fierce. In January 1944, a supposedly easy victory for the Allies had turned into a near disaster. The prize was Rome, Italy's capital, which the Germans had captured soon after Mussolini was deposed. (See Nazi Daredevil, page 38.) Now the Allies wanted the city. But no matter how hard the U.S. Fifth Army tried, they couldn't break out of their beachhead south of Rome. Many Allied soldiers were dead or wounded.

Anzio was a difficult situation that required an exceptional solution. Fortunately, an elite regiment of soldiers with unique abilities was available: the First Special Service Force. The Force, as they liked to call themselves, was made up of the toughest of the tough: rugged, independent Americans and Canadians who before the war had been outdoorsmen such as hunters, lumberjacks, forest rangers, and northern woodsmen.

The Force arrived in Anzio to fight alongside the Fifth Army in early February, and it wasn't long before Forcemen were terrifying the enemy. At night, with blackened faces, they sneaked into the nearby enemy camps to listen to the Germans' conversations and estimate their numbers. Sometimes the Forcemen stole things, like a pair of shoes, to let the Germans know they had been there. Other times they left something behind. Occasionally they killed one or two of the enemy in their sleep, and left threatening notes like "The worst is yet to come!" Afraid—very afraid—the Germans called them the Black Devils.

Even during their free time, Forcemen weren't ones to behave like other troops. By day, the Forcemen looked more like farmers than soldiers. They had discovered Borgo Sabotino, an abandoned village in no man's land, and decided to move in. There, instead of eating army rations, they raised chickens and cattle, and cultivated acres of cabbages and potatoes. It was definitely more comfortable than a bivouac!

Even in a Force full of characters, Sergeant Tom Prince—an Aboriginal from Manitoba, Canada—stood out. Growing up as a hunter on a reserve, he had learned many of the basics needed by a commando. He was especially good at tracking the enemy, observing

BEACHHEAD: the land taken on an enemy's shore, captured to protect future landings of soldiers and supplies

BIVOUAC: a temporary camp with little shelter

NO MAN'S LAND: the space between the front lines of opposing armies

THE FORCE

The First Special Service Force (also known simply as the Force) was a hand-picked unit of rough-and-ready American and Canadian paratroopers. Formed in July 1942, the Force's original task was to parachute into Nazi-occupied Norway and cause as much havoc for the Germans as they could. This seemed like the perfect mission for a group of guys with a reputation for stirring up trouble.

But first they needed to learn how to get along among themselves. Most of the troops were disorderly, and when they began training together

Continued on page 60

ALLIES AT ANZIO

When the Black Devils arrived at Anzio, everyone stationed there was part of VI Corps of the Fifth Army, under the command of Major General John P. Lucas. The Allied forces consisted of:

- ✪ 3rd Infantry Division (U.S.)
- ✪ 1st Infantry Division (U.K.)
- ✪ 46th Royal Tank Regiment (U.K.)
- ✪ 751st Tank Battalion (U.S.)
- ✪ 504th Parachute Infantry Regiment (U.S.)
- ✪ 509th Parachute Infantry Battalion (U.S.)
- ✪ 2 Commando battalions (U.K.)
- ✪ 6615th Ranger Force (Provisional) (U.S.)
- ✪ 45th Infantry Division (U.S.)
- ✪ Combat Command A of the 1st Armored Division (U.S.)
- ✪ 1st Special Service Force (U.S./Can.)
- ✪ 168th Brigade of the 56th Division (U.K.)

and their supporting units.

The beachhead at Anzio, Italy, in 1944. Buildings are damaged and Allied ships are anchored in the harbor.

Continued from page 58

at a military base in Montana (a western state on the U.S.–Canada border), they didn't like each other much. What's more, the rowdy Canadians soon found out just how much the townspeople in a bar near the military base also disliked them. A brawl broke out in the bar and—much to the amazement of the Canadians—American Forcemen came to their rescue! Forcemen from both countries were docked half a month's pay, but it was worth it: from then on, the Force worked as a team.

Instead of disbanding when the original mission to Norway was canceled, the Force was sent to the Aleutian Islands just off the coast of Alaska. Enemy Japanese had landed on the island of Kiska. By the time the Forcemen got there, though, the Japanese were gone. What a disappointment for guys who liked action! Happily for them, the Force's third assignment was for real. Anzio, Italy, was where they earned the nickname Black Devils.

After Anzio, the Force was sent to southern France, where their kind of fighting—close-quarter combat against numerically superior forces—was unappreciated by higher-ups. The Force was disbanded and each Forceman was ordered back to a unit from his own country. Their final day together was a sad one. When the order "Fall out the Canadians" was given, the Americans, with tears in their eyes, left gaps in their lines to honor the Canadians who had once been a part of their close-knit team.

The First Special Service Force shoulder insignia

Sergeant Tom Prince

German positions, and surveying landscape formations. He was also an excellent marksman and very brave.

During one battle, Prince volunteered to establish an observation post in an abandoned farmhouse. First he had to run a telephone line about a quarter of a mile ($\frac{1}{2}$ km) from his post back to the Allied artillery, so that from the farmhouse he could observe Axis troop movements and then send back exact locations. Telephone contact was good for a while, but all of a sudden communications were cut off.

Prince figured out what had happened: German shellfire had cut the phone wire. It took courage to save the day, and Prince had plenty of that. He stripped off his uniform and changed into clothes left behind by the farm's owner. Then, acting like an angry farmer who had remained on his land despite the war that raged around him, Prince went out into the field shaking his fists and shouting at the German line and then at the Allied line. Next, in plain view of the enemy, he grabbed a hoe and pretended to work the field. Secretly, he was following the telephone line to where the break had occurred. How nerve-racking! What if the Germans shot him?

At last he discovered the break, bent down, and pretended to tie his shoe while actually splicing the line together. For added effect, he continued to work the field before going back to the farmhouse to relay more information. Success! Thanks to his bravery, Allied artillery destroyed four enemy positions. Prince certainly deserved the Military Medal he was awarded later.

It was men like Prince and the rest of the Force who helped the Allies to fight their way from Anzio, through the mountains, and finally to Rome on June 4, 1944. The Forcemen were the first Allied troops to enter Rome, an honor that many Allied commanders had wished for. Losing Rome was a psychological blow for the Germans: they had thereby lost the capital city of one of the Axis powers.

IN THE NICK OF TIME

Nobody likes to be punished, especially when being cooped up is the penalty. But what if someone imprisoned you and your family, and you hadn't done anything wrong—you had simply been in the wrong place at the wrong time?

That's what happened in the Philippines in January 1942. Japan had declared war on the United States, and the American-controlled Philippines (islands in the Pacific Ocean southwest of Japan) had suddenly become a Japanese target.

The attack on the Philippines took many by surprise, trapping more than 2,000 Americans, Canadians, Europeans, and Australians. Prisoners of war! Men, women, and children were confined in a prison camp at Los Baños University, 25 miles (40 km) southeast of the Filipino capital, Manila. A barbed wire fence erected by the Japanese restricted the prisoners to the university grounds, and they were also denied radios and newspapers. In fact, the prisoners had hardly enough food to stay alive and often ate anything they could find, even frogs, rats, and dogs.

In February 1945 (more than three years after the prisoners were captured), American troops under General Douglas MacArthur began retaking control of the Philippines. Finally, the time seemed right to rescue the prisoners at Los Baños, still some 25 miles (40 km) behind enemy lines.

At last, a stroke of luck! A recent escapee from Los Baños gave American troops vital information to make the rescue a success. He handed over diagrams of the camp indicating where off-duty Japanese guards stored their guns, as well as a daily schedule of camp activities, pointing out the perfect time for an attack—7 a.m., when most guards participated in calisthenics … without their weapons!

On February 23—when most of the Japanese guards were about to exercise, sentries were changing the guard, and the prisoners were lined up for morning roll call—paratroopers from the 11th Airborne Division launched the raid, jumping from C-47s into a drop zone inside or near the camp.

Once on the ground, the paratroopers raced across

CALISTHENICS: *fitness exercises like jumping jacks*

DROP ZONE: *an area where troops land, usually by parachute*

GENERAL DOUGLAS MACARTHUR

MacArthur was a brilliant U.S. army general, best remembered for his commitment to defending the Philippine Islands from Japanese expansion during the Second World War.

MacArthur had been an excellent student, graduating first in his class at West Point (the U.S. Military Academy) in 1903. Later, in the First World War, he proved to be an outstanding leader as well. In fact, the then U.S. Secretary of War called him the best American front-line general.

Between the wars, he was superintendent of West Point and in 1925 became the youngest U.S. major general. In 1930, he was promoted to Chief of Staff of the army, but he stepped down five years later to become a field marshal and commander of the newly formed army of the Philippines' semi-independent Commonwealth government.

When it looked like the Japanese would force the U.S. troops in the Philippines to surrender in early 1942, U.S. president Roosevelt ordered MacArthur to escape to Australia and assume the duties of Supreme Allied Commander, Southwest Pacific. In Adelaide, Australia, MacArthur told reporters: "I came through and I shall return." And in 1944 he did. He was given the Medal of Honor, the highest award for gallantry in the U.S. military. On September 2, 1945, MacArthur accepted the official Japanese surrender.

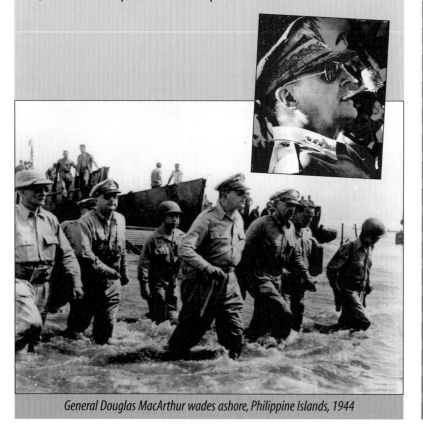

General Douglas MacArthur wades ashore, Philippine Islands, 1944

the camp to the weapons rack before the off-duty guards could react. Los Baños was under attack from three sides, and a number of the guards were hiding, fleeing for the hills, or dead.

As you can imagine, the prisoners were jubilant! But they were also confused. The attack had happened so quickly. Some were afraid to leave their huts; others wanted to retrieve personal items. Then someone yelled, "Enemy tanks!" Talk about chaos! Luckily, the "tank" noise wasn't the enemy at all. It was the U.S. army's 672nd Amphibian Tractor Battalion heading to the camp to help the prisoners escape. Fifty-four amphibious tractors (amtracs) had crossed Laguna de Bay, a freshwater lake two miles (3.2 km) from Los Baños. (See Amtracs, page 64.) On reaching the camp, the lead vehicle smashed through the gate and the others followed.

After about an hour, the camp was still in upheaval. Distant gunfire indicated that the combat team on their way to cut off any Japanese reinforcements was still at least three hours away. Meanwhile, thousands of Japanese troops were within striking distance. The prisoners needed to evacuate quickly.

The commander of the amtrac battalion ordered his men to set fire to the camp. This was so that the prisoners would move away from the barracks towards the main gate, where amtracs were waiting. Troops cleared the

AMTRACS

What looks like a tank but swims like a duck? An amphibious tractor. In the mid-1930s inventor Donald Roebling built his first "Alligator" amphibious tractor for search and rescue in the swamps of Florida. It had a hull like a boat and tracks like a tank. The U.S. Marine Corps soon recognized the value of such vehicles to carry troops and supplies from ships offshore to the beach and beyond. In addition, amtracs, as they were now called, could climb over offshore coral reefs that stopped conventional landing craft. By 1941 the first amtracs were rolling off the production lines of the Food Machinery Corporation. (FMC continued to produce armored vehicles into the 1980s.)

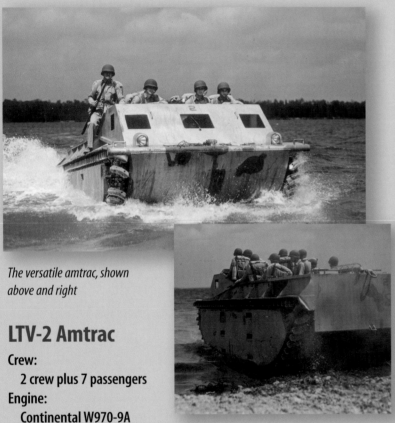

The versatile amtrac, shown above and right

LTV-2 Amtrac

Crew:
  2 crew plus 7 passengers
Engine:
  Continental W970-9A
  250-horsepower petrol engine
Weights:
  24,255 lb. (11,000 kg) unloaded, 29,263 lb. (13,271 kg) loaded
Dimensions:
  26.1' x 10.7' x 8.2' (7.975 m x 3.25 m x 2.5 m)
Maximum speed (land):
  20 m.p.h. (32 k.p.h.)
Maximum speed (water):
  7.5 m.p.h. (12 k.p.h.)
Armament:
  0.5-inch and/or 0.3-inch machine guns

barracks in advance of the fire and carried out more than 130 people who were too weak or sick to walk. The youngest rescuee reportedly was a three-day-old infant girl, carried out in a soldier's helmet-liner. Prisoners poured into the loading area. Those who could do so had begun the two-mile walk to the shore of Laguna de Bay, while others who were unable to make the hike were loaded aboard amtracs for the journey. In the distance they could hear guns firing, the enemy getting closer.

By 11:30, the evacuation was complete and the camp was totally in flames, but it was still critical to get the prisoners to safety quickly. The first shuttle of approximately 1,500 prisoners had left the beach at about 10 o'clock, the amtracs sliding into the lake for the two-hour journey from danger. Several amtracs were fired on by Japanese, but only one had to off-load its cargo of evacuees and be towed to safety.

Seven hundred prisoners had to stay behind and wait for the amtracs to return. This was terrifying, as Japanese troops were closing in. Luckily, the amtracs escaped in the nick of time. The only casualty among the prisoners was one woman who was grazed by a bullet.

The raid on Los Baños was one of the most successful of all time.

CODES AND CIPHERS

During the Second World War each side eavesdropped on the other's radio messages. To disguise their words, both the Axis and the Allies used ciphers and codes.

If you know that "10-4" is police radio talk for "affirmative," then you already know what a code is. Codes replace complete words or phrases with groups of letters, numbers, or symbols. To encode (scramble) or decode (unscramble) a message, the sender and receiver need to know the same code or have identical code books.

Ciphers are different. A cipher replaces one letter with another letter using either a simple or a complex system. If you received an enciphered message that read KHOS, what would the sender be trying to tell you? In this case, each letter in the alphabet was replaced with a different letter that was three positions (letters) to the right. Your sender wanted—HELP. KHOS is the cipher text and HELP is the plain text. The sender and the receiver must use the same key, or the receiver cannot decipher (unscramble) the enciphered (scrambled) message.

Simple ciphers have been used for thousands of years, but by the Second World War many messages were written in complex systems worked out by machines. Code breakers were busy!

Some battles were won at least partly because one side knew ahead of time what the other was planning. Sometimes code books and keys were discovered when an enemy was captured, but more often codes and ciphers had to be broken. Among the trickiest for the Japanese to solve were messages sent by the Navajo code talkers, U.S. Marines who spoke a kind of Navajo slang that only another Navajo code talker could understand. Meanwhile, the cracking of two complicated Axis cipher machines kept the Allies on their toes: the infamous German Enigma and the challenging Japanese Purple. Code breaking drastically changed the course of the war.

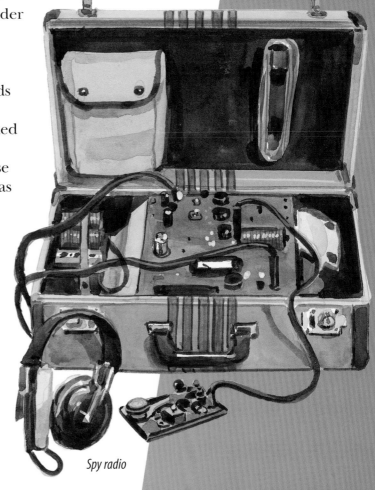

Spy radio

GREAT
BRITAIN

Bletchley Park •

London •

FRANCE

ENIGMA MACHINE

The Enigma machine looked a lot like a typewriter in a wooden box. Each machine had a keyboard, a display board with letters that lit up, a plug board that looked something like an old telephone switchboard, and notched rotors.

By the end of the Second World War, each machine had a choice of five rotors, each of which was wired differently. But on most machines only three rotors were installed at a time (the German navy had a special version that used four rotors at once). It could be any three in any order, and these settings were changed daily.

To encipher a message, a code clerk typed plain text into the Enigma machine. As the clerk pressed a key, electric current passed through the plug board, then through each rotor, to a reflector disk. The disk sent the current back through the rotors and plug board to the display board, where a letter lit up. Another clerk recorded the new, lit letter. This was the cipher text.

Each key pressed advanced the first rotor one position. When the first rotor rotated once all the way around, the second rotor advanced one position. When the first rotor rotated a second time, the second rotor advanced one more position. This went on until the second rotor rotated all the way around once. Then the third rotor wheel advanced one position. Because the rotors kept stepping up,

Continued on page 68

ULTRA HUSH-HUSH

Every country has its secrets … especially when it's at war. During the Second World War, one of the best ways to discover the enemy's secrets was to eavesdrop on their radio transmissions. Messages were sent in Morse code by wireless radio to the intended receivers, but any listening station surrounded by forests of antennae could pick up a message as long as it was tuned to the frequency on which the message was sent. So, receiving a message was easy; reading it was the hard part. The text was usually enciphered and looked like a jumble of letters. If the key to the cipher was unknown, the message was unreadable. Code breakers were needed.

Great Britain's code breakers worked at Bletchley Park, the government code and cipher school north of London. At the beginning of the war, approximately 120 people worked there, but by the end there were more than 7,000. Even though a lot of people worked at Bletchley Park, the goings-on there were secret. Code breakers couldn't tell anyone about their work. Imagine going somewhere every day without being allowed to tell your family and friends what you are doing there!

Radio communications could be enciphered by hand or by machine, but machines usually enciphered the important messages. The British used the Typex cipher machine while the Americans used SIGABA. The Germans had the incredible Enigma machine, an elaborate mass of plugs, rotors, and wiring. Many high-placed Germans believed that even if the Allies captured an Enigma machine, they would not be able to break the cipher. And they had good reason to be confident: the most advanced version had a possible 15 billion billion settings. Plus, the settings were changed often— usually every day. What headaches the Bletchley Park code breakers must have gone home with!

By the time the Second World War broke out, the Enigma had already been around for two decades, although the Germans had continued to improve it during that time. Dutchman Hugo Koch had invented the Enigma machine in 1919, but he didn't realize his machine's true potential. He sold it to a German engineer named Arthur Scherbius, who did. The

Continued from page 66

the same letter pressed repeatedly would result in a different letter on the display each time.

Once the entire message had been typed into the Enigma and every letter that had lit up had been recorded, the cipher text was handed to an operator to transmit by radio in Morse code.

The Enigma machine at the receiving end had to be set up exactly the same way as the one at the sending end. A clerk there typed the cipher text into the Enigma machine and the plain text message lit up letter by letter.

A Women Accepted for Volunteer Emergency Service (WAVES) stands in front of a code-breaking machine called a Bombe.

Rotor indicators show the operator which positions the rotors are in.

Rotors scramble the letters a different way each time.

Lights indicate the cipher text when enciphering.

Keys are used to type the plain text when enciphering.

MORSE CODE: a system that replaces letters and numbers with dots and dashes for visual messages, or with long and short sounds for audible messages

engineer developed and refined it, named it Enigma, and then sold the idea to the German government. By the late 1920s, the German military were using it. Immediately, code breakers in Great Britain, France, Poland, and other countries tried to break the cipher. All were frustrated.

Finally, in the early 1930s, the Polish Cipher Bureau obtained an out-of-date Enigma machine. True, it lacked essential parts then being used by the German military, but it did clue them in to how the Germans were enciphering their messages.

Soon after that, a German officer looking for easy cash sold two key documents to the French: an operating manual for the Enigma and several encryption keys to Enigma ciphers. This could have been an amazing break for the French, but they didn't know how to use the information. Neither did the British. Fortunately, the French passed it on to the Polish Cipher Bureau. This was the missing piece of the puzzle the Poles needed. Once they understood the Enigma's wiring, they used clever reasoning to limit the number of possible keys. Then some tedious trial and error led to successfully cracking the code!

By early 1933, Polish code breakers were reading the German air force's version of the Enigma. But deciphering

Enigma messages by hand was time-consuming. To speed up the process, they built a machine called a Bombe that reduced the odds for finding each daily Enigma setting. The Bombe worked well until the summer of 1938, when Polish code breakers suddenly found they could no longer read Enigma-enciphered messages. The Nazis had improved the Enigma machine by adding two more rotors.

Fearful that the Germans were about to attack their country, Polish code breakers invited British and French representatives to a meeting in Warsaw, where the Poles divulged what they knew about military Enigma. They also gave Britain and France each a replica Enigma machine. Soon, code breakers at Bletchley Park were working hard to break the new five-rotor air force Enigma, as well as the naval version of the machine that was wired differently.

During the early stages of the war, the British captured Enigma machines, rotors, and code books from sinking U-boats and ships. They also improved the Bombe using cribs (common phrases likely to be found in a message, like the lines "To the group" and "Nothing to report"). Disks inside the Bombe rotated to check every disk combination. The Bombe stopped moving at any setting at which the crib was possible. Only the possible settings needed to be hand-tested.

The improved Bombe plus the lucky finds helped Bletchley Park code breakers decipher Enigma information, which the Allies code-named Ultra. By 1943, the Allies were regularly reading German naval messages. Stealing Enigma rotors or code books was now forbidden, because if the Germans thought the British could crack their cipher, they would change it.

Spy organizations have a tradition of not revealing information, so Ultra remained a secret until the early 1970s, despite being the greatest intelligence coup of the war.

PURPLE, MAGIC, AND BARON OSHIMA

Instead of using rotors like the Enigma machine, the Japanese cipher machine—code-named Purple—had a series of electromechanical stepping switches. It was the equivalent of the Germans' four-rotor Enigma machine with a typewriter on each side. If you guessed that Purple wasn't as portable as the Enigma, you are right.

By September 1940, the U.S. Signal Intelligence Service (SIS) had built a machine that acted like Purple. Chief Signal Officer General Mauborgne often called his cryptanalysts magicians, so any intelligence they gathered was called Magic. The Americans gave the British a copy of Purple in early 1941, but it was usually the Americans who deciphered Purple and the British who deciphered Enigma.

Although Purple was mainly a diplomatic code, it still yielded valuable information the Allies could use. Baron Oshima, the Japanese ambassador to Berlin, communicated often with his home government using Purple. In November 1943, Oshima toured German fortifications along the Atlantic coast facing Britain. His report sent back to Japan described the defenses in great detail. This was indeed helpful information for the Allies, who intercepted the message.

A second intercepted message revealed that in May 1944, Hitler was fooled by British deception experts into believing that the Allies would create many diversions during the invasion of France but strike with their main force in the Pas de Calais, after a smaller attack on Brittany and Normandy. How very encouraging for the Allies! Because Hitler hadn't guessed the true Allied strategy, the D-Day invasion (see D-Day, page 78) would have a good chance of succeeding.

A MOST SECRET SOURCE

Naples

ITALY

MEDITERRANEAN SEA

TUNISIA

LIBYA

Alexandria

El Alamein · Cairo

SUEZ CANAL

EGYPT

A Spitfire, shown behind two huge aerial cameras, before taking off on a reconnaissance mission, 1944

AERIAL RECONNAISSANCE

Planes have been used for spying on the enemy ever since the First World War. Every major nation had bombers and transport planes between the First and Second World Wars, and modified versions of these were used for reconnaissance. They flew at high altitudes so that observers could see large areas all at once.

During the Second World War, as radar improved and fighter planes were developed that could fly as high as the reconnaissance planes, it became safer to fly reconnaissance missions at lower altitudes, where there were no radar waves to detect them. Missions were flown in modified fighters, which allowed the crew to zip away from any enemy aircraft that spotted them.

For moving targets such as ships at sea, reconnaissance continued to use high-flying aircraft so observers could check out large areas.

The Germans were giving away many of their secrets … and they didn't know it. The Nazis were sure their cipher was unbreakable, but the British had figured out how to read their messages. (See Ultra Hush-hush, page 66.) Naturally, the Allies intended to protect their source. If the Germans knew that the Allies had broken their cipher, they would change it. On the other hand, if the Germans continued to use the current one, the Allies might be able to gather enough intelligence to gain the advantage.

In 1941 and 1942, the Allies fighting in North Africa needed an edge. The Afrika Korps seemed to be always one step ahead of the Allies. (See Rommel and the Afrika Korps, page 72.) Rommel was amazingly clever, but just when it seemed he could overrun the British, the war turned. Rommel had a problem he could not control: the Afrika Korps lacked adequate supplies. Food was scarce, fuel and ammunition were low, and equipment needed fixing. At the same time, the British had just received ample supplies and new reinforcements. Convoys of supply ships sent from Italy were Rommel's only hope to sustain the Afrika Korps. (See Hoodwinked, page 54.)

The strategy should have worked, except the British knew about Rommel's problem and figured they also knew how to make it worse. What a gift for the Brits!

To make sure the Afrika Korps was fully informed of what was happening, German reports of the convoys' departures, routes, and destinations were sent to Rommel using the "unbreakable code." And, yes! the British intercepted the messages, pinpointed the

MARTIN MODEL 187 BALTIMORE

The Martin Baltimore developed from the Martin Maryland, a bomber used by the French air force and then by the RAF after France surrendered. Part of 69 Squadron at Malta (responsible for maritime reconnaissance over the central Mediterranean) flew Baltimores.

Baltimore II

Crew:
    4
Engines:
    2 Wright Cyclone GR-2600-A5B
Weight:
    24,000 lb. (10,900 kg) loaded
Dimensions:
    48.5' x 14.2' (14.8 m x 4.32 m), 61.4' (18.7 m) wingspan
    Maximum speed (at 11,620'/3,540 m): 303 m.p.h. (488 k.p.h.)
Armament:
    12 x .30-inch machine guns (four fixed forward-firing in wings, two in dorsal [top] mount, two in ventral [belly] mount, four fixed aft-firing in fuselage)
    2,000-lb. (907.19 kg) bombs

ROMMEL AND THE AFRIKA KORPS

When the Second World War broke out in Europe, North Africa also became a battlefield. (See The Desert War 1941–42, page 43.) Libya had been an Italian colony since 1912, and Mussolini dreamed of enlarging his empire. When Italy declared war on the Allies in June 1940, Italian troops began moving eastward across North Africa towards the British-controlled Suez Canal—the waterway in Egypt that connected the Mediterranean Sea with the Red Sea. Of course, the British fought to push the Italian soldiers back into Libya.

When the Italians started to lose, in February 1941, Hitler sent them help: a German armored unit called the Afrika Korps, commanded by Erwin Rommel. Soon the British were calling Rommel the Desert Fox because he was so wily and quick that he had driven the Allies back to the Egyptian border in three brilliant offensives.

By June 1942, Rommel had forced the British back to El Alamein, an Egyptian seacoast town just 50 miles (80 km) west of Alexandria. The British headquarters in Cairo was in a panic. They even burned classified documents to keep them from falling into German hands. Refugees fled eastward—but they need not have worried. Lack of supplies and reinforcements had stymied the Afrika Korps. Meanwhile, the British were gaining strength: troops, supplies, and equipment poured into El Alamein. The war was turning around again. In late 1942, the British Eighth Army forced Rommel to retreat westward.

When the British succeeded in sinking the convoys trying to reach Rommel, the Afrika Korps was faced with defeat. Rommel was evacuated back to Germany, and the rest of the army was captured by the Allies. Although Rommel was now disenchanted with Hitler, he commanded German forces that faced the Allies on D-Day. In October 1944, he was implicated in a plot to assassinate Hitler. Rather than face a trial, he committed suicide by drinking poison.

General Rommel, Libya, 1941

tankers and cargo ships, and then sank them. Rommel's troops became desperate, but still the Germans did not suspect how it was that the British were finding all the convoys. Apparently it never occurred to them that the enemy was reading their messages, and this was partly because the British were so cagey! Once they knew a convoy's route, they would send out a reconnaissance plane that just happened to fly over the ships. The plane always made sure that sailors spotted it so the Axis would assume the attacks were based on the plane's report.

The system didn't always work perfectly. On one mission, the British striking force showed up where Ultra said a convoy would be . . . but there was no convoy. It had been delayed and was still on its way. What made an embarrassing mistake into a nerve-racking problem was that the attacking British ships were spotted by German aircraft. The British eventually hunted down the convoy, but what would happen if the Germans realized they had been expecting it? Would they change all their codes?

Luckily for the Allies, the Germans refused to believe the Enigma machine's cipher had been broken. Whenever the British seemed to have prior knowledge of Axis plans, the Germans tended to blame the leak on their Italian allies, whom they considered incompetent or indiscreet. Alternatively, they chose to believe that the secrets had been discovered by British spies.

THE ALLIED WAR AT SEA

The Battle of the Atlantic was bloody. It lasted from September 1939 to May 1945—almost as long as the entire Second World War. For the British, however, September 1939 to May 1943 was the grimmest part, because during that three-and-a-half-year period Germany tried its best to cut the British off from needed fuel, food, and military supplies. Britain was an island that imported most of its food and resources. So, the idea was to starve the British into submission … and the Nazis very nearly did just that.

On September 4, 1939—the day after Great Britain declared war on Germany—a U-boat (German submarine) sank the passenger liner *Athenia*. Already, the Atlantic was unsafe! But the situation grew much worse. When Germany occupied France in the spring of 1940, the German navy based many submarines in French ports. This gave the Germans direct access to the Atlantic and allowed U-boats to range farther out to sea and stay there longer.

U-boats in the Atlantic were controlled from Lorient, France, on the Bay of Biscay. There, Befehlshaber der U-boote (BdU) received radio communications from U-boats giving their locations, sightings, and sinkings. BdU, headed by Admiral Karl Dönitz, responded with intelligence reports and orders. The British intercepted many German naval messages, but anything enciphered by the Enigma machine was still a mystery to them.

Meanwhile, U-boats were creating havoc on the North Atlantic. They were hunting in groups called "wolf packs," which meant they spread out in patrol lines to look for ships. When one of them found a target, they all came together to attack. The British sent ships in convoys protected by armed escorts, but there were only so many escorts available. Some escorts could accompany convoys only to the middle portion of the transit. There they turned around and escorted other convoys back to Britain. As you can imagine, U-boats

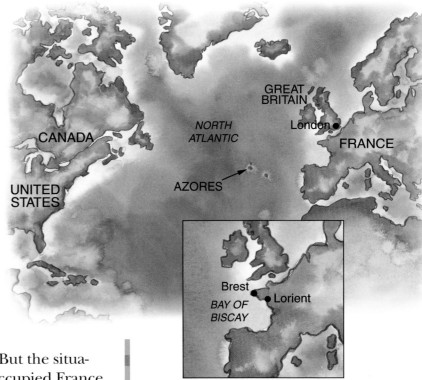

BdU: the German navy head-quarters that gave orders to U-boats in the Atlantic and Indian oceans

COMMANDER RODGER WINN

During the Second World War, many of the most successful British workers in military intelligence were civilians. Commander Rodger Winn is a good example. Before the war, Winn had been a successful lawyer, frustrated because an attack of polio had prevented him from achieving his boyhood goal of joining the Royal Navy. As a civilian, however, he was allowed to become an assistant to the head of the Submarine Tracking Room—the strategic core of the war against U-boats. He was so good at his job that he was eventually promoted to head. But because it was unprecedented for a civilian to direct such a vital military organization, he was made a commander in the Royal Navy Volunteer Reserve (RNVR).

Inside a U-boat

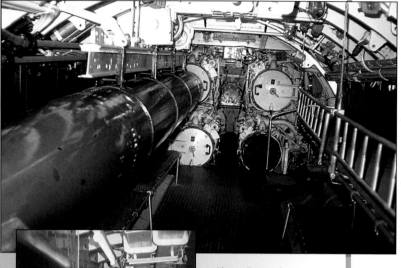

Above: Forward torpedo room

Left: Petty officers' (non-commissioned officers') bunks showing railings and round hatchway to the control room

Above: Radio room

Right: The galley. Note the railing around the edge of the stove to stop things falling off.

had a field day tracking unescorted or poorly escorted convoys beyond the range of air patrols. When a U-boat sighted a British convoy, it signaled its position to BdU and waited for orders. When the order was given, the wolf pack converged on the ill-fated ships.

By the early summer of 1941, the Royal Navy had good news: the naval Enigma was broken. Finally, the British knew where the U-boats were, where they were going, and what they expected to find there. The deciphered messages —code-named Ultra—were sent to the Submarine Tracking Room at the Operational Intelligence Centre (OIC) in London, where the British monitored the world's oceans. There, Ultra was combined with intelligence from a wide variety of other sources, including medium- and high-frequency direction-finding equipment, other radio intercepts, and reconnaissance reports. Now the OIC map of deployed German submarines was probably as current as the one at BdU headquarters!

Convoys were rerouted and wolf packs were attacked. When OIC warned convoys to change their routes, the information was made to look as if it came from some other source, such as a direction-finding fix or aerial reconnaissance. The actual source— Enigma decrypts—was always kept secret. Unfortunately, U-boats still sank convoys, sometimes because the warning came too late and other times because convoys didn't have enough fuel to take a longer route. However, in 1941 many more merchant ships made it to their destinations.

Then, in early 1942, there was suddenly something wrong: U-boats were sinking many more merchant ships than they had the year before. In December 1941, the Germans had

When watched over by scout planes, relatively few convoys were successfully attacked by U-boat wolf packs.

Merchant ship viewed through an attacking submarine's periscope

broken Navy Cypher #3, the cipher used by British and American Atlantic convoys. But the broken cipher wasn't obvious for months, because for the first half of the year many of the sinkings happened in North American waters, where the Allies were less careful about security.

Meanwhile, in February 1942, the Germans introduced a new four-rotor Enigma machine. Atlantic U-boat messages, code-named Shark by the British, were now unreadable. Again, OIC had to rely on other forms of intelligence. At least there was one bright spot: the British already knew how Dönitz thought and how U-boats operated.

By the end of 1942, British fuel supplies were perilously low. Just in time, the British had a breakthrough. On December 13, they were able to read their first U-boat "Shark" message. Almost immediately they read messages which indicated that Cypher #3 had been broken. Mystery solved. By the next summer, Cypher #5 was in place, and the Germans never cracked this one.

In April and early May 1943, more than 500 Allied merchant ships made it across the Atlantic, while 45 German U-boats were sunk. Dönitz must have been frustrated. On May 23, 1943, he reassigned most of his U-boats to an area southwest of the Azores. A few remained in the North Atlantic to try to fool the Allies into thinking the wolf packs were still there.

In the end, the Nazis never succeeded in severing British supply lines. OIC and Ultra saw to that. But U-boats fought to the very end of the war in Europe, sinking their last victim on May 7, 1945, the day Germany surrendered.

GERMAN RAIDERS

During the early years of the war, Germany attacked Allied merchant ships with surface warships as well as U-boats. Some were large warships such as heavy cruisers or battleships, but others were armed merchant ships modified to carry guns. They blended in with regular traffic on the high seas and attacked lone Allied vessels. The most famous German commerce raiders were the battleship *Bismarck* and the large cruiser *Graf Spee*.

THE SINKING OF THE *BISMARCK*

The *Bismarck* was Germany's pride and joy, a powerful and speedy warship. Heavily armed and armored, it set out on its maiden raid in May 1941 to hunt for and destroy convoys. The British battle cruiser *Hood* chased the German warship, but a lucky shot fired from the *Bismarck*'s 15-inch (38 cm) guns plunged through her deck armor to penetrate a magazine. The *Hood* exploded. The 20-minute battle was a stunning victory for the Germans.

But hold on! The *Bismarck*'s fuel tanks had taken a hit and she was leaking precious fuel. Eventually, the ship's captain headed south to Brest, a port on the western coast of France. The Royal Navy spotted her and a torpedo-bomber made a lucky strike, jamming the *Bismarck*'s rudder so the ship could only turn left. She circled helplessly for a while, then turned north—straight into Royal Navy units. The *Bismarck*'s fate was sealed. Soon she was a blazing wreck. Torpedoes finished her off, and she rolled over and sank. This was Germany's last surface raid into the Atlantic.

OTENCIA MARÍTIMA ALEMANA

Bismarck *(German battleship, 1940–41)*
This photo was printed in a Spanish publication in1941 and was obtained by the U.S. naval attaché, Madrid, whose stamp appears on the left.

THE BATTLESHIP *BISMARCK*

KMS *Bismarck*
Crew:
  2,092–2,192
Dimensions:
  824' x 118' x 30.5' (251 m x 36 m x 9.3 m)
Speed (max.):
  29 knots (nautical miles per hour)
Armament:
  8 x 38 cm guns (four twin turrets)
  12 x 15 cm guns (six twin turrets)
  16 x 10.5 cm anti-aircraft guns (eight twin turrets)
  16 x 3.7 cm and multiple 2 cm anti-aircraft guns

THE SUPER SECRET SCRAMBLER

CANADA

UNITED
STATES

NORTH
ATLANTIC

AZORES

GREAT
BRITAIN

London ●

FRANCE

The Nazis were eavesdropping. They were listening in on conversations between the American president and the British prime minister. Although the transatlantic radio-telephone link was supposedly protected at each end by an A-3 Scrambler that changed intelligible speech into gibberish, the Germans heard everything that Roosevelt and Churchill talked about … everything they said over the link between the fall of 1941 and the spring of 1944. They also overheard phone calls made by other senior staff who used the link to discuss important matters.

And everyone at that time had plenty to talk about, such as the war in Africa, the war in the Pacific, the invasion of Europe, and the shape of the post-war world. Roosevelt and Churchill liked the connection because they could speak person to person, without having to go through layers of diplomatic and military bureaucrats. They also liked it because they could talk normally— their conversations did not need to be encoded or decoded. Instead, a scrambler on the talking end mixed up the voice frequencies so the words sounded like gibberish. On the hearing end, the message was unscrambled, turning the garble back into intelligible English. Both leaders thought the link was secure enough, but they still used security-conscious words just in case someone did intercept their calls. As a further precaution, the transmission frequencies were changed often, making the scrambler even more secure.

But—believe it or not—an American journalist had broken the secret of the A-3 Scrambler in the fall of 1939. An article appeared in the *New York Times* that said the American ambassador to France had used the link to call Roosevelt when the Germans invaded Poland.

CIPHONY: voice transmission scrambled electronically

D-DAY: the Allied invasion of Normandy on June 6, 1944, which led to the liberation of France and the invasion of Germany

Scramblers

Voice scramblers alter the human voice, which consists of high, medium, and low tones. The A-3 Scrambler changed each tone so that its pitch was higher or lower. For example, the high tones might sound low or in the middle range, while the low tones might sound high. The results no longer sounded like words.

The story even pinpointed where one scrambling device was located: in a soundproof room under the White House. Some secret! Now everyone who read the *Times* knew about the scrambler, including a German spy living in New York. He clipped the story from the newspaper and sent it to Germany.

As it turned out, the A-3 Scrambler was not difficult for the Germans to figure out. Developed by American Telegraph and Telephone Company in the late 1930s, the scrambler was considered state of the art, but it was based on 1920s technology. Engineers at Deutsche Reichspost didn't have an A-3 Scrambler, but it didn't matter. All they had to do was listen to the messages over and over in order to develop their own version of the device.

By September 1941, the Germans had built a giant receiving antenna on the coast of occupied Holland. Soon they were intercepting Allied conversations and sending transcripts directly to Heinrich Himmler, head of the SS. (See Schutzstaffel, page 39.) Himmler passed the information on to Hitler.

Listening for signals was a 24-hour-a-day job. German operators had to pay attention at all times because Churchill had a habit of telephoning in the middle of the night. But it was worth it. Twice the Nazis learned critical information through the A-3 Scrambler link that affected their war plans.

The first big news came just after the fall of Mussolini in 1943. (See War-weary, page 54.) At the time, Hitler wasn't sure if Italy's new prime minister intended to remain Germany's ally. However, a Roosevelt–Churchill conversation made it clear that the Allies were negotiating for Italy to surrender. Based on this information, Hitler sent 12 German divisions into Italy to join the 8 that were already there. When the Italians surrendered, they were quickly disarmed by the Germans. And when the

FRANKLIN DELANO ROOSEVELT

FDR—as Franklin Delano Roosevelt was commonly known—was president of the United States for twelve years (1933–45), longer than any other U.S. president. This is particularly remarkable because in 1921 he was partially paralyzed by polio, a disease that damages muscles. Through exercise, he regained strength in his back, arms, and hands. But to walk he still needed braces.

FDR had conquered his personal tragedy, polio. During the Great Depression (1929–41) he proved that he wanted to help down-and-out Americans conquer their tragedies: lost jobs, hunger, and hopelessness. In his first presidential inaugural address, in 1933,

President Roosevelt signs the declaration of war against Japan, December 8, 1941.

he boldly declared: "The only thing we have to fear is fear itself." Under FDR's leadership the federal government worked towards making the United States a prosperous nation. During his "fireside chats"—radio broadcasts to the nation—he explained actions his government had taken and what he expected to happen in the near future.

In 1939, when German armies seized Poland, FDR's focus began to change. He was worried about German aggression. He was also concerned about Japanese expansion. Even before America joined the war, FDR corresponded often with Churchill. Many members of Congress thought FDR was a warmonger; they did not want to go to war. But in early 1941, the U.S. Congress did pass the Lend-Lease Act, whereby the U.S. could lend or lease war supplies to the Allies at a low cost. It was a way for America to help the Allies without actually entering the war. Of course, when the Japanese bombed Pearl Harbor in December 1941, many Americans changed their mind and were now eager to fight the enemy.

Eighty-two days after he was sworn in for his fourth term as president , FDR died. Harry Truman took over as president.

Allies landed on the Italian peninsula, they were astonished to find that the Germans controlled most of Italy. (See Hoodwinked, page 54.)

The Germans learned the second crucial piece of information on May 5, 1944. In a five-minute conversation, Roosevelt and Churchill discussed the invasion of Europe. Their words seemed to imply that the invasion, D-Day, would happen soon ... very soon. In fact, the invasion was launched on June 6, 1944, only a month later.

The D-Day information was the last significant intelligence the Germans learned by eavesdropping on the A-3-protected conversations. Shortly thereafter, Deutsche Reichspost noticed a decline in the number of signals being sent through the A-3 system. They figured the United States and Great Britain must be using another connection. And they were right. The Allies were switching to the Green Hornet, a more secure ciphony system. The Green Hornet (officially called SIGSALY) earned its nickname from the buzzing sound it made when someone tried to eavesdrop. The buzz sounded very much like the theme song of a then popular radio show called ... you guessed it ... *The Green Hornet.*

SIR WINSTON LEONARD SPENCER CHURCHILL

When Winston Churchill was young, he was so restless and energetic that he drove many people crazy. He also appeared to be dim-witted. In fact, he was at the bottom of his class ... the very bottom. No one would have guessed he would one day become an accomplished writer, a talented painter, and—most astonishing of all—prime minister of Great Britain.

In his late teens, Churchill entered military college. It took him three tries to pass the entrance exam. But finally his life seemed to turn around when he took two subjects he really liked—tactics and fortifications. He was good at them!

Winston Churchill, 1944, raises his fingers high in his famous "V" for Victory sign.

Churchill began his career as a soldier. His adventurous spirit took him to Cuba as an observer with the Spanish, who were trying to quell a revolt. There he wrote several newspaper articles. His stories were good. He soon took leave from his regiment to be a war correspondent from various British colonies. In 1899, while reporting on the Boer War in South Africa, the Boers (Dutch settlers) captured and imprisoned him. He became famous after he wrote about his daring escape. He returned home a hero, decided to run for a House of Commons seat in the British Parliament, and won. He worked enthusiastically to do his best in any parliamentary position he was appointed to.

During the 1930s, Churchill tried to convince the rest of Parliament that the Nazis were dangerous. He was concerned about the German military buildup. Other politicians called Churchill a warmonger until Hitler proved the Nazis really were a threat.

Churchill became prime minister in May 1940 and held the position until July 1945—most of the Second World War. He is famous for saying: "I have nothing to offer but blood, toil, tears, and sweat." Actually, he also offered his heroic spirit. Even when the odds seemed to be against Great Britain, he raised British spirits by lifting his fingers high in a "V" for Victory.

When his party lost the first post-war election, he stayed in Parliament. But he now had more time to lecture, paint, and write. Between 1948 and 1953, he wrote an authoritative six-volume history of the Second World War. During some of that period, he also found time to serve a second term as prime minister, from 1951 to 1955. After that, he managed to finish the four-volume *History of the English-Speaking Peoples* that he had begun in the 1930s. He remained a member of the House of Commons until a few months before he died, in 1965.

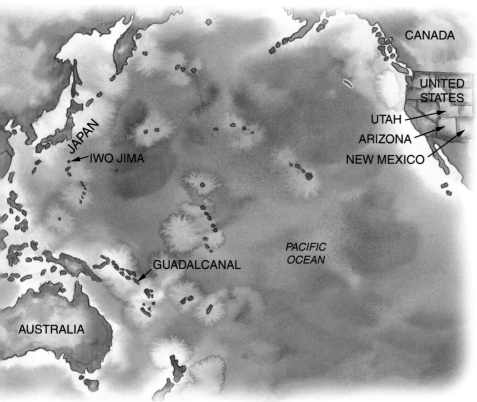

The Japanese were baffled. The code used by the U.S. Marines sounded like gibberish. Usually the Japanese were good at cracking U.S. codes, but this one was exasperating! It didn't even help that many of the code breakers had been educated in the U.S. and were familiar with American expressions and everyday slang.

In fact, there was a good reason for the Japanese bewilderment. The code was not based on English at all, but on a rare language spoken by the Navajo—Native Americans who live in parts of Arizona, Utah, and New Mexico. For the Marines, the code was a dream come true: it was fast, accurate, and almost impossible to crack. They liked it so well that they used it from 1942 to 1945.

Most codes used during the Second World War required cipher machines. Sending and receiving coded messages was so complex that American military leaders complained about the time it took. Whenever a message was sent, someone had to type it into a cipher machine to turn it into secret text then pass it on to a radio operator for transmission. At the receiving end, someone had to write the secret text down then pass it to a code operator to type into his cipher machine, which turned it back into readable text. The system worked, but it took too long!

Then, in early 1942, Philip Johnston, an engineer living in Los Angeles, came up with an idea. He was a First World War veteran and believed that the Navajo language, which he had learned as a child, could be developed into a spoken code. It was certainly a rare language. In the early 1940s the Navajo language wasn't written down and only

GUADALCANAL

Guadalcanal, the largest of the Solomon Islands, is located in the southwest Pacific Ocean, northeast of Australia. The Japanese occupied the island early in the war, and by the summer of 1942 were building an airfield from which about 60 bombers would menace the South Pacific. In August, the Americans began fighting land, sea, and air battles to force the Japanese to evacuate. The Japanese finally fled Guadalcanal in March 1943.

IWO JIMA

Iwo Jima is a small island south of Japan. During the Second World War, the Japanese used it as an air base from which fighter planes attacked American bombers. In February and March 1945, the Americans fought for the island and won. Six Navajo code talkers worked around the clock for the first two days of the battle, sending and receiving more than 800 messages, all without error. Major Howard Connor, 5th Marine Division signal officer, said, "Were it not for the Navajos, the Marines would never have taken Iwo Jima."

about 30 non-Navajo could speak it. None of them were Japanese.

Johnson was so sure of his idea's workability that he approached the Marines. Four Navajo showed the commanding general of Amphibious Corps, Pacific Fleet, that they could encode, transmit, and decode a three-line English message in just 20 seconds. At that time, cipher machines took 30 minutes to do the same job. The general was impressed!

Soon, 29 Navajo recruits began developing a code for military purposes. They did this with four basic points in mind. First, each code word was connected logically to the term it stood for to make it easy to memorize. For example, owls have good eyesight, so the Navajo word for owl (*ne-as-jah*) meant "observation plane." Second, the words were descriptive. For instance, they called a destroyer a shark (*ca-lo*). Third, every code word was as short as possible, to save time. And fourth, the code makers avoided words that could easily be confused with other words.

Next, they invented an alphabet code for words that didn't have a code word, such as place names. For each English letter, they chose a word that started with that letter and then substituted the Navajo word. For example, Nagasaki—the Japanese city—was spelled N–nut, A–ant, G–goat, A–ant, S–sheep, A–ant, K–kid, I–ice. It was spoken *nesh-chee, wol-ach-ee, klizzie, wol-ach-ee, dibeh, wol-ach-ee, klizzie-yazzie, tkin.*

As complicated as the Navajo code looks, it's even more confusing to listen to because the Navajo speak in four tones: high, low, rising, and falling. The same syllable spoken in a different tone means something totally different, which is one reason the Navajo language is very difficult for adults to learn.

Complicated, yes, but when an experienced cryptographer looked over the list, he suggested a way to make the code even harder for the Japanese to crack. Since so many words

Navajo code talkers on an island in the Pacific

MISTAKEN FOR JAPANESE

The Navajo have dark skin and hair, high cheekbones, and little facial hair, so Americans on the front lines sometimes captured code talkers, mistaking them for Japanese spies. Indeed, some Navajo were nearly shot for wearing U.S. Marine uniforms. A few divisions assigned each of their code talkers a non-Navajo bodyguard. There are those who say the bodyguards were assigned to protect the code talkers; others claim they were really protecting the code and were under orders to kill any code talkers who were about to fall into enemy hands.

had to be spelled out, he was afraid the repetition of the Navajo equivalents for certain letters might help the Japanese decipher the code. He recommended that the 12 letters used most often (A, D, E, I, H, L, N, O, R, S, T, U) have three equivalents. This meant that the *N* in the word *Nagasaki* could be the Navajo word for needle, nut, or nose, while the *A*s could be the word for ant, apple, or ax. This addition to the code turned out to be a brilliant idea. It really confused the Japanese, because a Navajo code talker could send the same message using different words.

Now the 29 recruits had to memorize 411 words. The recruits were drilled again and again. They would have to send and receive messages quickly, so there was no time for hesitation. And no mistakes were allowed, because one mistranslated word could lead to tragedy.

In August 1942, when the first code talkers joined Marine units stationed in the South Pacific, it was not an easy transition. Initially, the spoken code caused almost as much confusion for American radio operators as for the Japanese, because they thought the enemy had taken over their radio frequency. And one commander exclaimed he didn't want code talkers on his ship unless they could out-race his cipher machine. Wasn't he surprised when the code talkers took less than five minutes to relay a message that normally would have taken two hours!

In November 1942, the code talkers proved their true worth at the Battle of Guadalcanal, an important victory for the U.S. that boosted American morale. Suddenly there weren't enough Navajo for every unit that wanted them. By the end of the war, more than 400 code talkers were serving with the U.S. Marines.

The Japanese never broke the Navajo code. For years, the military forbade the code talkers from telling anyone about their wartime duties. Decades later, President Reagan officially recognized the code talkers for their part in defeating the Japanese at Guadalcanal, Iwo Jima, and other key battles by declaring August 14, 1982, Code Talker Day. In 2001, the original 29 were awarded Congressional Gold Medals. The code talkers who followed them received Congressional Silver Medals.

SAMPLE CODE WORDS

Code word	Navajo word	Navajo meaning
America	ne-he-mah	our mother
battleship	lo-tso	whale
bomber plane	jay-sho	buzzard
corps	din-neh-ih	clan
February	woz-cheind	squeaky voice
minesweeper	cha	beaver
South America	sha-de-ah-ne-hi-mah	south our mother
submarine	besh-lo	iron fish
torpedo plane	tas-chizzie	swallow
village	chah-ho-oh-lhan-ih	many shelter

AMBUSH AT MIDWAY

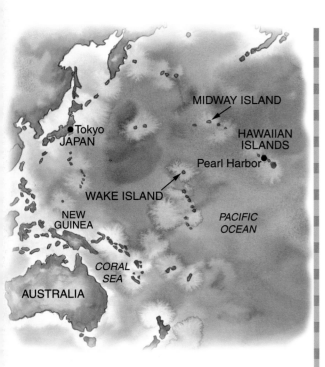

The American military had a secret: they had cracked the Japanese Purple-machine cipher. (See *Purple, Magic, and Baron Oshima*, page 69.) Japan was quickly expanding its empire in Southeast Asia and the southwest Pacific in the 1930s and early 1940s, and the Americans were watching closely. Purple hinted that the Japanese might attack the United States ... but where? Tension was building. Intercepting and decoding Purple's messages would help the Americans figure out where the Japanese were planning to strike.

Suddenly, an alert! The next Japanese target might be an American naval base in the Pacific Ocean. But which base? And when? The Japanese had been very cagey—their radio messages gave few details. The U.S. military issued a general warning to all U.S. bases in the Pacific, but they were still guessing the date and target when, on December 7, 1941, enemy bombers attacked the headquarters of the U.S. Pacific Fleet at Pearl Harbor in the Hawaiian Islands. Japanese bombers and submarines seemed to have come out of nowhere. What a blow! Most of the U.S. fleet was damaged or destroyed.

In spite of his enormous victory, Admiral Isoruku Yamamoto, commander-in-chief of the Japanese fleet, was worried. No aircraft carriers had been in the Hawaiian harbor during the attack, so the Americans were still free to prowl the Pacific Ocean and counterattack. And time was on the Americans' side. Yamamoto knew Japan could win a short war, but he believed the Americans would win if the war lasted more than 12 months. Japan had only enough fuel to fight for a few months and had counted on stunning the U.S. into a quick negotiated peace. Instead, the bombing of Pearl Harbor ignited American passions, and on April 18, 1942, the U.S. sent the Japanese a warning: 16 B-25s bombed Tokyo. The physical damage was minimal, but the bombing lifted U.S. spirits ... and frightened the Japanese, who until then had thought they were safe from attack.

Machines like Purple were expensive, so the Japanese navy used a manual code, which the U.S. called JN 25, to send most of its messages. Hypo—the navy's radio intelligence organization in Hawaii—was intercepting

MIDWAY

Midway is an atoll, two islands about six square miles (1,550 ha) in area surrounded by a lagoon enclosed in a coral reef. Located in the Pacific Ocean 1,136 miles (1,828 km) northwest of Hawaii, Midway is the outermost link of the Hawaiian chain. In 1935, an American airline started using it as a base for flights between the U.S. and Asia. It became a U.S. naval air station in August 1941.

DAMAGE AT PEARL HARBOR

AMERICAN LOSSES
2,403 people killed
188 aircraft destroyed
4 battleships sunk
1 minelayer sunk
1 training ship (former battleship) sunk
15 ships damaged

JAPANESE LOSSES
64 people killed
29 aircraft destroyed
5 midget submarines destroyed

Admiral Yamamoto

JAPANESE EMPIRE, 1942

Japan began building an empire when it invaded Manchuria (northeastern China) in 1931. The League of Nations (which resembled a weaker version of today's United Nations) condemned Japan's aggression but didn't take action. Soon it became clear that the Japanese military wanted to control more of Asia. When the Second World War broke out, most of the world's attention was diverted to what was happening in Europe. The Japanese government decided this was a great time to expand south and east, where there were countries rich in raw materials such as oil and rubber. But the United States stood in their way. Japan bought most of its oil from the Americans. When the U.S.—wary of Japanese expansionism—decided to reduce the amount of oil it would sell to Japan, in 1941, Japan strengthened its alliance with Germany and Italy.

In March 1942, the Japanese were feeling confident. They had practically demolished the U.S. Pacific Fleet and had conquered areas in Southeast Asia and the South Pacific that were rich in valuable resources such as oil, rubber, tin, and bauxite. The only goal they hadn't reached yet was taking the Philippines—but that would happen soon.

messages in this code. In April they discovered that the Japanese were planning an assault code-named MO. Did MO stand for Port Moresby? If so, the Japanese might use this New Guinea port on the Coral Sea as a base from which to capture the rest of New Guinea and threaten Australia. The Americans couldn't afford to be surprised again. Instead, they needed to surprise the Japanese!

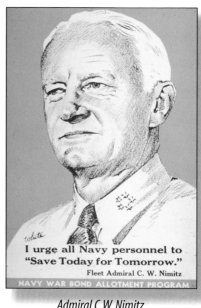

Admiral C.W. Nimitz

This time Hypo gathered enough information for U.S. Pacific Fleet commander Admiral Nimitz to mount a successful counterattack. Technically, the Battle of the Coral Sea was a draw—one carrier sunk and one damaged on each side. But actually it was a strategic victory for the U.S. because, for the first time during the Second World War, the Japanese were turned back. The battle also proved that Hypo could provide accurate and timely intelligence.

At about the same time, Hypo uncovered another Japanese operation. Intercepted messages revealed that the target was called AF. Hypo thought AF was the U.S. naval base on Midway. (See Midway, page 86.) Admiral Nimitz agreed, but Op-20-G—the navy's radio intelligence organization in Washington—wanted to be sure. After all, if the Americans sent the fleet to the wrong place, the Japanese could take the real target unopposed.

The code breakers at Hypo came up with a clever plan to determine whether or not Midway was the target. By means of an underwater telegram cable between Pearl Harbor and Midway never tapped by the Japanese, Midway was told to send an uncoded radio message to Pearl Harbor saying their water-distilling plant had broken down. The Americans hoped the Japanese would report this information in a message using the

USS Yorktown *at the Battle of Midway, June 1942*

AIRCRAFT CARRIERS

An aircraft carrier is a ship with a runway on top. Under the runway is a hangar deck for storing aircraft, and beneath the hangar deck is the ship's hull. The "island" beside the runway is where sailors work while aircraft take off and land. Each carrier is protected by anti-aircraft guns and by planes used only to guard the carrier. All three American carriers at the Battle of Midway were of the same design: the Yorktown class, named after the first ship launched in that class. They each carried 80 aircraft. The Japanese carriers were of three different designs, each carrying 60 to 70 aircraft.

Yorktown-class Carrier

Yorktown (CV-5), *Enterprise* (CV-6), and *Hornet* (CV-7) fought at Midway. *Yorktown* was sunk there.

Crew:
   1,890
Dimensions:
   809.8' x 83.26' x 21.5' (246.74 m x 25.37 m x 6.55 m)
Maximum speed:
   37.4 m.p.h. (60.2 k.p.h.)
Armament:
   8 x 5-inch dual-purpose (anti-aircraft and anti-surface ship) guns
   Up to 96 aircraft

TBF Avenger torpedo bombers flying in formation. The Battle of Midway was the first time Avengers were used in combat.

CODE NAMES

The German military used code names in the First World War to disguise what was being written or talked about. During the Second World War, code names were still used to confuse the enemy. The Americans and British developed separate lists but co-ordinated them to make sure none of the 10,000 words appeared on both. At the beginning of the Second World War, the Japanese numbered their operations or used alphabetical code names such as MO or MI. By the end of the war, they had switched to nouns and adjectives like other nations.

Today, operation names are no longer classified. Sometimes a code name is released to the media even before the mission begins.

code AF. Sure enough, after the Midway broadcast, a Japanese intercept station on Wake Island reported that AF was short of water!

Nimitz stationed army bombers on Midway and ordered all submarines there to leave. Piecing together bits of information, Hypo further discovered that the Japanese were sending almost their entire fleet to Midway. Nimitz would need everything he had to counter. All available U.S. carriers headed for Midway: *Hornet, Enterprise,* and *Yorktown.* The Japanese had no inkling they had lost the advantage of surprise.

Early on June 4, 1942, the Japanese made the first strike, bombing Midway. The bombers returned to their carriers but American bombers followed them from Midway. The Japanese realized that they needed a second strike against the island. Since they believed there were no American ships in the vicinity, the Japanese ordered their bombers remaining on the carriers—which had been reserved for assaulting possible U.S. ships—to replace their torpedoes with bombs for the second land strike. Then a shock: scouts spotted the U.S. fleet! The change-bomb order was canceled, but the torpedo bombers could not take off because their own bombers returning from Midway were still landing. What a terrible nightmare!

The situation became even more complicated when U.S. bombers took off from the American aircraft carriers. The Japanese carriers, with bombs and torpedoes scattered all over their decks, were easy targets. All four Japanese carriers were sunk.

Yamamoto had been planning to destroy the entire American carrier fleet once and for all. He had chosen a target the U.S. would be sure to defend, trying to lure every U.S. aircraft carrier into a battle where the Japanese could ambush them. Instead, the Japanese themselves were ambushed.

Hypo's decoded messages had given the U.S. the edge. Until Midway, Japan had always been the attacker and the Americans the defender. Now the Americans took the offensive … for the rest of the war.

The following is an excerpt from an incredible but true tale of British deception against their German foes. Check out the full story in HOODWINKED: DECEPTION AND RESISTANCE

(Publication date: February 2004.)

Weapons, manpower, strategies—to win battles, countries at war muster everything they can, not just in the field but also behind the lines. Often the most effective weapon is a fighter's intelligence. *Hoodwinked: Deception and Resistance*—second in the series Outwitting the Enemy—is a collection of Second World War stories about soldiers and civilians who used unconventional methods to outsmart their foes.

DEAD RINGER

Tricking the enemy into believing a lie can be nerve-racking—not to mention dangerous. One tiny slip-up and … *zap!* the project is botched. Every invented fact must be believable and every detail must fit perfectly with the rest, especially if a blunder could cause your side to lose lives.

During the Second World War, the Allies and the Axis tried to outmaneuver each other. One of the most successful British deceptions was Operation Mincemeat, carried out in 1943. The Allies (including British, American, and Canadian troops) had just defeated the Axis (mainly German and Italian troops) in North Africa. The next battleground seemed obvious to many: the island of Sicily off Italy's southwestern coast. (Sicily was the closest Axis-held land across the Mediterranean Sea from North Africa.) The trick was to convince the Axis that the Allies were going to attack Greece and Sardinia instead.

Creating the ruse was a lot like writing a movie script in which a corpse plays the leading role. But the British could control only the first few scenes and had to hope like crazy that the players on the Axis side would perform their parts as the British predicted, producing a successful ending for the Allies.

First the British had to find the main character. Coming up with any old dead body would be easy enough (after all, this was wartime), but finding the right corpse was a challenge. The perfect leading man needed to be a slightly out of shape thirty-something—able to pass for a staff officer in the Royal Marines (a credible courier of secret information). It had to appear that his plane had crashed, he had drowned, and his body had been washed ashore. What's more, he needed a family willing to release his body to the military, no questions asked— everything had to be kept top secret.

Could the British pull this deception off without a hitch, or was the idea impractical and doomed to failure?

If you are interested in finding out more about the stories in *Ultra Hush-hush*, go to the Annick Press Web site: **www.annickpress.com**.

ACKNOWLEDGMENTS

Many thanks first of all to Sheryl Shapiro, for guiding the project from its earliest stages to completion. David Craig's attention to detail always impressed me. His pictures are a wonderful addition to the stories. I am grateful to Sandra Booth of Annick Press, who sought out the photographs from around the world that grace these pages. I am sincerely thankful to John Sweet. Special thanks go to Professor Wesley K. Wark of the University of Toronto, who agreed to review the manuscript. Any errors or omissions are of course mine alone. Finally, I am indebted to Tina Forrester for doing a wonderful job of bringing these stories to life.
—Stephen Shapiro

For my family.
—S.S.

Thanks to Michael Martchenko, and a special thanks to Travis Craig for his assistance with the maps. And lastly, my thanks to the team who worked on this book who made it so enjoyable for me.
—David Craig

Sincere thanks to the many people and organizations that helped make this book possible:
• To creative director Sheryl Shapiro, who put the book together ever so carefully—juggling text, artwork, and photos—so that each section of the book is a cohesive unit yet flows smoothly into the next.
• To artist David Craig, whose superb paintings make the stories come alive.
• To Professor Wesley K. Wark, Department of History, the University of Toronto, who—even though extremely busy—read over the manuscript and suggested changes, additions, and deletions.
• To researcher Sandra Booth, who searched long hours for the many photos that amplify information in the stories and sidebars.
• To Guy Bastiaens of Fort Eben-Emael, Cristiano D'Adamo of the Web site Regia Marina Italiana, and Ron Wise, for supplying technical consultation and images.
• To Gábor Hopocky, John Byrd of Big Sky Enterprises, and Tracy Dungan of V2 Rockets.com, for supplying images.
• To Mrs. Taconis for permission to use the Kryn Taconis photograph on page 5.
• To Gudmundur Helgason, curator of uboat.net.
• To Pfc. Gehrke of the 82nd Airborne Division and Bonnie Henning of the Institute of Heraldry for their efforts—although fruitless—to obtain permission to use the 82nd Airborne insignia.

I would especially like to thank co-author Stephen Shapiro, who has shared his astonishing wealth of knowledge about the Second World War with me. Stephen chose all the stories in this book and was always available to answer my questions. What a storehouse of knowledge he has!
—Tina Forrester

For Tom, who supports my love for research and writing.
—T.F.

BIOGRAPHIES

Stephen Shapiro (Toronto) developed an interest in military history at a young age. He has spent the last 15 years avidly immersed in the study of warfare. His passion for the strategies and nuances of military maneuvering during the Second World War has inspired him to share his interest. Stephen is a recipient of the Canadian War Museum History Award.

Tina Forrester (Toronto) is a researcher and writer on a broad spectrum of subjects. Her previous works for Annick Press include the co-authorship of *The Millennium Time Capsule Book* and contributions to *I Touched the Moon, By Truck to the North*, and *Hidden Worlds: Amazing Tunnel Stories*.

Illustrator **David Craig** (Toronto) is highly skilled at depicting historical events and people. His previous works include the dramatic illustrations in *Attack on Pearl Harbor*, and *First to Fly: How Wilbur and Orville Wright Invented the Airplane*.

PICTURE CREDITS

4, NARA NWDNS-26-G-2343/Department of Transportation, U.S. Coast Guard, Office of Public and International Affairs.

5 left image, based on Kryn Taconis/National Archives of Canada/PA-169940

5 upper right image, 44, based on Strathy Smith/Canada Dept. of National Defence/National Archives of Canada/PA-132785

5 lower right image, *Yank Magazine*/Library of Congress, Prints & Photographs Division, FSA-OWI Collection, LC-USE6-D-009109 DLC.

8, NARA NWDNS-80-G-413988/ Joe Rosenthal, Associated Press/Department of Navy, Naval Photographic Center

9, NARA NWDNS-306-NT-3163V/New York Times Paris Bureau Collection

10, back cover, NARA NWDNS-200-SFF-52/PK Hugo Jger/Jerome R. Lilienthal

11, NARA NWDNS-44-PA-82/Essargee/Office for Emergency Management, Office of War Information, Domestic Operations Branch, Bureau of Special Services

12, NARA NWDNS-44-PA-230/Siebel/OEM, OWI, DOB, BSS

16, Special thanks to John Byrd of Big Sky Enterprises for supplying the image of the Iron Cross 2nd Class

20, NARA NWDNS-306-NT-3157V/U.S. Information Agency/Photographic File of the Paris Bureau of the New York Times

22 upper image, AWM negative number 006872

22 lower image, AWM negative number 006868

24, Special thanks to Ron Wise for providing the image of the 1940-48 pound banknote

25, NARA NWDNS-80-G-205686/Department of Defense, Department of the Navy, Naval Photographic Center

31, 32, Special thanks to Guy Bastiaens, of Fort Eben-Emael, for supplying the five photographs of the fort and for much technical consultation

34, Ufficio Storico della Marina Militare, Rome, Italy (historical division of the Italian navy)

34, 35, 37, Special thanks to Cristiano D'Adamo, of the website Regia Marina Italiana, http://www.regiamarina.net, for supplying the images of Durand de la Penne, the ARO—Oxygen Rebreather, and the Italian Gold Medal of Valor

38, National Archives, courtesy of USHMM Photo Archives #81963

39, Courtesy of USHMM Photo Archives #24532

40, NARA NWDNS-242-EB-7 (38)/Eva Braun Collection

46 upper image, Geoffrey Keating/AWM negative number 007070

46 lower image, Geoffrey Keating/AWM negative number 007069

50 left image, NARA NWDNS-208-N-43888/Office for Emergency Management, Office of War Information, Overseas Operations Branch/New York Office, News and Features Bureau

50 right image, NARA NWDNS-77-BT-187/War Department, Office of the Chief of Engineers, Manhattan Engineer District

53, U.S. Naval Historical Center photograph/"Meine Kriegserinnerungen auf Schlachtschiff *Scharnhorst*," page 19

56, NARA NWDNS-80-G-54412/Department of Defense, Department of the Navy, Naval Photographic Center

57 upper image, AWM negative number SUK14622

57 lower image, Special thanks to Tracy Dungan of V2 Rockets.com for supplying the image of the German radar Wurzburg

59, AWM negative number 305157

60 upper image, based on J.J. Schau/Canada. Dept. of National Defence/National Archives of Canada/PA-128264

60 lower image, Special thanks to John Byrd of Big Sky Enterprises for supplying the image of the First Special Service Force shoulder insignia

62 upper image, NARA NWDNS-26-G-3584/Department of Transportation, U.S. Coast Guard, Office of Public and International Affairs

62 lower image, NARA NWDNS-111-SC-407101/Department of Defense, Department of the Army, Office of the Chief Signal Officer

64 upper image, back cover, Alfred T. Palmer/Library of Congress, Prints & Photographs Division, FSA-OWI Collection, LC-USE6-D-005514 DLC

64 lower image, Alfred T. Palmer/Library of Congress, Prints & Photographs Division, FSA-OWI Collection, LC-USE6-D-005512 DLC

68, The Mariners' Museum, Newport News, VA.

69, NARA NWDNS-64-M-276/General Services Administration, National Archives and Records Service, Office of the National Archives

70, AWM negative number SEA0063

72, NARA NWDNS-242-EAPC-6(M713a)/General Services Administration, National Archives and Records Service, Office of the National Archives

74, Special thanks to Gábor Hopocky for supplying the four photographs of the interior of the U-995 submarine taken at Laboe

76, Official U.S. navy photo/Library of Congress, Prints & Photographs Division, FSA-OWI Collection, LC-USE6-D-008870 DLC

77, U.S. Naval Historical Center photograph/U.S. Naval Attache, Madrid

79, NARA NWDNS-79-AR-82/Abbie Rowe/Department of the Interior, National Park Service

81, based on National Film Board of Canada. Photothèque/National Archives of Canada/C-071095

83, NARA NWDNS-127-N-82619/Sgt. James L. Burns/Department of Defense, Department of the Navy, U.S. Marine Corps

88 left image, NARA NWDNS-44-PA-371B/OEM, OWI, DOB, BSS

88 right image, NARA NWDNS-44-PA-1039/OEM, OWI, DOB, BSS

89, U.S. Naval Historical Center photograph/Official U.S. navy photograph

90, NARA NWDNS-80-G-427475/Department of Defense, Department of the Navy, Naval Photographic Center

GLOSSARY

ABWEHR: the German Military Intelligence Service and espionage organization

ALLIES: the alliance during the Second World War that included Great Britain, France, Australia, Canada, India, New Zealand, South Africa, the United States, and many other nations

AMBASSADOR: a government's official representative in another country

AMPHIBIOUS: refers to a vehicle that can operate both on land and in water

AXIS: the alliance during the Second World War that included Germany, Italy, Japan, Finland, Hungary, Bulgaria, and Romania

BATTALION: an army unit of roughly 500 to 1,000 men, usually divided into three companies

BEACHHEAD: the land taken on an enemy's shore, captured to protect future landings of soldiers and supplies

BELLIGERENTS: countries at war

BIVOUAC: a temporary camp with little shelter

BLITZKRIEG: the German word for *lightning-war* that describes the speed with which German armies conquered foreign nations

BRIGADE: an army unit of roughly 3,000 to 7,000 men, usually divided into three battalions

CASEMATE: a reinforced enclosure in which artillery is mounted

CONVOY: ships escorted by other ships for protection

CUPOLA: a rounded structure that houses a gun

D-DAY: the Allied invasion of Normandy on June 6, 1944, that led to the liberation of France and the invasion of Germany

DETACHMENT: a group of soldiers deliberately separated from their unit for some purpose

DIVISION: an army unit of roughly 10,000 to 20,000 men, including all sorts of support staff, and usually divided into three brigades

GREAT BRITAIN: England, Scotland, and Wales

MI5: (also known as the Security Service) stands for Military Intelligence, section 5. It's a government organization responsible for British national security and counter-espionage. The Double Cross Committee grew out of MI5.

MI6: (also known as the Secret Intelligence Service, or SIS) stands for Military Intelligence, section 6. It's a government organization responsible for gathering outside of Great Britain any intelligence that concerns British vital interests.

NAZI: a member of the National Socialist German Workers' Party. Nazis believed in a strong centralized government headed by a leader with absolute power.

NEUTRAL: a country not at war

NO MAN'S LAND: the space between the front lines of opposing armies

PANZER: the short form of the German word for *tank, panzerkampfwagen,* which means "armored fighting vehicle"

RECONNAISSANCE: a look at something to gain information

SOE: (Special Operations Executive) the British agency responsible for sabotage, resistance, and other sorts of unconventional warfare in Axis-controlled territory

U-BOAT: German submarine (short for *Unterseeboot,* which means "undersea boat".)

UNIT: a group of soldiers who live, train, and fight together. Units can range in size from four men to more than 100,000.

UNITED KINGDOM (U.K.): the shortened name for United Kingdom of Great Britain and Northern Ireland, made up of England, Scotland, Wales, and Northern Ireland.

INDEX